Amazon Alexa - The Complete User Manual to Amazon's AI Assistant

Tips, Tricks and Skills
for Every Amazon Alexa Device

by C.J. Andersen

Contents

Introduction

Hello and welcome! Thank you for buying this Alexa user guide and I look forward to sharing my knowledge and helping you to master your new Amazon device. Before we get under way I would like to make a couple of suggestions.

Firstly, I would like to encourage you to get familiar with Amazon's Help Pages (https://amzn.to/2IObbJu) and here's why... Amazon is constantly tweaking, updating and expanding the capabilities of both its devices (Fire tablets, Fire TV, Echo, Echo Dot, Echo Show etc) and its AI software Alexa.

And when I say constantly, I mean ALL the time.

Amazon seem to be on a mission to add Alexa to everything! As I write this, Amazon has just announced the release of an Alexa device for the car (Echo Auto) and a new Alexa-enabled microwave, so it's a safe bet that Alexa will continue to grow and expand into many other areas over the coming months and years.

While I will continue to publish updated editions of this guide, I want to be sure that anyone who has bought this book has the chance to stay up to date with the frequent changes and Amazon's help pages for your device is the best place to do that. When changes to the way your device works or new features are introduced, the information is also updated on these help pages. Personally, I don't find their help pages super user-friendly, but nevertheless they are the best place to stay up to date with changes and improvements.

Secondly, I wanted to say a word about this guide, how it has been put together and the best way to use it. Of course, you should feel free to dip into a particular chapter if there is some specific information you are looking for, but I would also urge you to read the book from start to finish as it follows a logical progression.

If this is your first Alexa-enabled device, then you will discover that the Alexa app is at the heart of everything you can do with your device. For that reason, I have laid out this guide to take you step by step through every option within the app starting at the top and working down to the bottom. It's really the easiest way to approach and master Alexa without jumping back and forth and getting lost in the numerous options.

I am confident that anyone, no matter what level their tech skills, will find learning and using Alexa pretty straight forward. If there's anything that you still find confusing after having read this guide then please email me at cjandersentech@gmail.com

Okay, let's go!

1: Introducing Alexa

It seems unlikely that there are many consumers left who haven't heard about Alexa, but for the uninitiated here is a quick recap. Alexa is the voice activated, cloud based Artificial Intelligence that provides you with a personal home assistant.

The idea behind Alexa is to make queries and home tasks simpler by only having to use your voice to get things done. Whether it be activating entertainment, getting the latest news or turning on your home lighting (or microwave!).

Alexa is far from the finished article, but you can already see the potential for Alexa to grow and become something like a voice activated replacement for Google search and many other tasks that until now require you to sit down at a computer or get up out of your chair and operate some other piece of household equipment.

In my household I mainly use Alexa to play music, find out movie show times, listen to my favorite radio stations, podcasts and audio books, set alarms and timers, operate my smart home lighting, check sports scores, make shopping lists, set reminders and ask a whole host of trivia questions that I want a quick answer to.

There are many more uses for Alexa and in this book you will learn which are the most useful and entertaining for you.

Using Alexa is easy to setup and not complicated to use, although some trial and error can be expected, however the challenge is discovering the many different things it/she can do. And this is why I wrote the guide, to give you a clear understanding of every different Alexa feature so you can choose and use the features most important to you.

For example, Alexa can recognize up to 10 unique voices in a household, which gives Alexa the tools to make sure kids don't add items to the shopping list or ensure only your calendar events are mentioned if you ask Alexa about your schedule! This is one of the many Alexa features that we'll explain and explore in this book.

But, before we go any further I should point out that in this guide I won't be showing you how to setup specific Alexa-enabled devices, although I will make it clear if a feature only works with certain devices. If you want to know more about a specific Amazon Echo device, then please take a look at the books I've already published. You can see them all here: www.amazon.com/CJ-Andersen/e/B076J91LB4

In this guide the focus will be on the Alexa App which is basically the command center for Alexa. You can access the Alexa App via your mobile phone, tablet, PC or Mac, and it is by becoming completely familiar with the App that you will be able to unlock the full potential of Alexa.

Downloading the Alexa App

So, before we get started, you will need to have access to the Alexa App and there are several ways to achieve this.

Preinstalled – If you have an Amazon Fire Tablet you will find that the Alexa App is already preinstalled. If for some reason you don't see the Alexa App on your Fire tablet, then navigate to the Amazon app store and download it. Here is a direct link: amzn.to/38KF1fI

Via your PC/Mac – You can access the Alexa App online by visiting alexa.amazon.com and logging in using your Amazon.com email address and password

Via your mobile phone or tablet - For mobile phones and other tablets visit the app store for your device and download it. Here are direct links for the Alexa App on iTunes and Google Play:

itunes.apple.com/us/app/amazon-alexa/id944011620

play.google.com/store/apps/details?id=com.amazon.dee.app

CJ's Tips: Frustratingly the Alexa App is not identical on different platforms. That is to say the layout, interface and some of the features are different depending on whether you're looking at the App on a PC or on a mobile phone. Throughout this book, where necessary, I will point out differences in the interface, but I strongly recommend using a mobile phone or tablet as that is the most popular way of accessing the Alexa App, and currently the best way to see all of the App's features.

2: Meet Alexa — The Alexa App Basics

For any voice command you read in this chapter be sure to use your wake word ("Alexa", "Amazon", etc) first.

So, let's get straight to it and start learning how to find your way around the Alexa App. We will refer to **Settings** several times here. They are a part of the App, but there's so much information to share about **Settings** that it has its own chapter. It's inevitable that some information will be covered in both places.

Amazon calls Alexa the "brain behind" their range of Echo devices and other 3rd party Alexa-enabled devices. Alexa is cloud-based, making it possible for Alexa to continually be improved and updated. If you're worried about security, consider that it's likely that many of your accounts are already somewhere in the cloud — banking, credit cards, medical in addition to other Amazon accounts such as Prime or Drive. The same level of security used with that information is used with Alexa.

The App, your Voice and the Screen

Most of what you can do via the Alexa App can also be done with voice. If you're listening to an Amazon music station, for example, you can select the Pause button on the App or simply say, "Pause." In the remainder of this guide, we will note things you cannot do by voice, such as Change the Wake Word. In all other cases, assume you can accomplish the task with your voice, and give it a try.

On some Alexa devices, such as the Echo Show, there is also interplay between the App and the device's touch screen. For example, when you add an item to your **Shopping List**, the list will appear for about 30 seconds on the Echo Show screen before reverting to its Default display.

In this guide, we will be looking mainly at using the Alexa App on your PC, Mac or mobile device and using voice control to maximize the potential of the App. If relevant, we will point out Alexa commands that generate screen interplays on Alexa-enabled devices.

Note on clarifying terms: In tech talk about devices, the terms "page" and "screen" are sometimes used interchangeably in a confusing manner. To be clear, in this guide, a "page" is a page on the App you can view on your phone, tablet or computer; the "screen" is a device's touch screen.

A Word About Help & Feedback

The *Help & Feedback* page, accessible within the Alexa App, is discussed in detail later, but it's worth knowing before we get started that this section contains a wealth of information about all the topics discussed throughout the rest of this book.

A Word About the Alexa App Layout

As you view the App layout on a PC or Mac, you'll see a Menu of App pages on the left and the current page on the right. That's what you might see on large mobile devices too, but on most phones and tablets, you will see just the current page; the *Menu* (aka More) icon will be depicted with three horizontal lines at the bottom left.

You will need to tap on this Menu icon to navigate to different pages of the App.

Note that on the tablet and mobile phone version of the App; no matter what page you are on, there are five icons at the bottom of the page:

- The *Home* icon to take you back to the *Homepage* which is a trapezoid shape with two lines under it, I think it's supposed to represent the Cards (more about those later).

- The *Communications* icon (a little speech bubble) to take you to the relevant pages of the App for making calls and sending messages.

- The *Play* icon, a circle with a triangle inside, which takes you to the *Music & Books pages*.

- The **Devices** icon (a little house with two switches inside) which takes you to the **Devices** page where you can access and manage the Amazon Echo devices and any other smart home devices that are integrated into your Alexa system

- The **Menu** icon (three horizontal lines) which takes you to a page showing all the other functions of the App, including **Settings**.

So let's start at the beginning and select the **Homepage** of the App.

The Alexa App Homepage on your PC or Mac

When you're on the **Homepage**, starting at the top, what you'll see are different sections which are **Things to Try**, your **Cards** and, when you're playing most media, a media Player at the bottom of the page will appear.

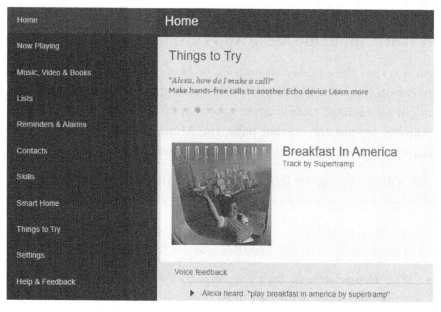

Things to Try: When on the **Homepage**, a **Things to Try** feature appears at the top. It rotates through some suggestions of things to say to Alexa related to current or trending issues.

There are shaded buttons below the suggestions. I click or tap manually through them since I don't have the patience to watch them rotate at the rate of 7–8 seconds per suggestion. Occasionally something of interest appears – recently I discovered that Alexa can talk like a pirate, which was pretty funny - but I've found they can be a time waster in the same way social media can be when there are other things I should be doing.

Cards: The next things you'll see after the Things to Try suggestions are your Cards. A Card is created with most verbal interactions with Alexa. The Card preserves the request and response from Alexa such as a music station or a forecast you requested, a recipe you've selected, a Skill used or items you added to your shopping list.

Cards form your Alexa Dialog History. You can scroll down the Cards to review them. A list of them is also available in Settings. Select **Settings**, and scroll down to the **General** section, and select **History**.

Card options: On the right of each Card you'll see the word More with a V-shaped icon, known as a caret. Click on it to see options for further action:

- **Remove card:** Select this to delete the card. Note that deleting your entire Card history at once is only possible by deregistering your device, something you'd likely do only if giving it away or selling it.

- **Give Voice feedback:** The Card will show what "Alexa heard" with the question, "Did Alexa do what you wanted?" Answering the question helps Alexa improve its understanding of how you speak. You don't have to answer the question, of course. If you answer "no," you'll be given the option to "Send more detailed feedback. Select that for unlimited space to provide feedback and the opportunity to request that Amazon get back to you on your input.

- **Learn More:** This takes you to Alexa and Alexa Device FAQs, which is a useful part of the **Help & Feedback** section of the menu; I recommend you browse it when you have a few minutes. To use these options on older Cards, select **More**, and the box will expand to show them.

Bing Search and Wikipedia: One or both these options might appear on a Card:

- **Search Bing:** If Alexa is unclear about what you say or if you ask about a person, place or thing, Alexa will provide the option to "Search Bing for..." whatever your query was about. Bing is your only search engine option on the App.

- **Learn more on Wikipedia:** Depending on the subject you ask Alexa about, the Card might give you a short answer and a link to the topic on Wikipedia.

- **Player:** When media (songs, radio, podcasts, etc.) is loaded, whether playing or paused, the *Player* appears at the bottom of the Alexa App, and allows you to control that media. The bar includes an icon of the current item in the queue. The Player appears at the bottom of the App regardless of what page you're on. It is discussed fully in the *Now Playing* section next.

The Alexa App Homepage on your mobile device

As mentioned earlier the Alexa App interface is quite different on a mobile compared to your PC or Mac; particularly the Homepage of the App on your mobile device looks very different.

What you'll see on your mobile device at the top is the **Talk to Alexa** icon on the left (tap on this to enable Voice Control via your mobile device); a **Question Mark** icon that leads to the **Help & Feedback** section on the right-hand corner; and a greeting (Good Morning, Good Afternoon etc...) in the middle.

Below the greeting you'll be able to scroll upwards through a series of floating tabs that either take you to different pages of the App, offer information on new Skills or Things to Try, or – once you've started using Alexa – will show links to where you left off on you Audible book or the Music currently playing/ or last played. These tabs act a bit like the Cards mentioned above.

However, to get the full options for your Cards via the App on your mobile device, then go to **Menu > Activity**.

As with the App on your PC or Mac, when you play any media via your Alexa device, the **Player** will appear at the bottom of your current page.

At the bottom of the Homepage of the App on your mobile device you'll see the icons mentioned earlier: the **Home** icon, the Communications icon, the **Play** icon, the **Devices** icon and the **Menu/ More** icon.

3: The Now Playing Page

For any voice command you read in this chapter be sure to use
your wake word ("Alexa", "Amazon", etc) first.

One of Alexa's most attractive features is its ability to play media from a wide range of sources, and we'll discuss all the options in greater detail later.

I appreciate that you might not have anything to play yet and therefore much of this chapter might not make sense to you right now. If this is the case, feel free to skip ahead and return to this chapter when you are ready.

Now, as we mentioned earlier, on some pages of the Alexa App there can be significant differences in the layout and interface when you view it on a tablet or mobile phone compared to a PC or Mac. The **Now Playing** page is one of these pages where it is quite different.

Basically it doesn't exist as an option in the **Menu** on the tablet or mobile phone version of the Alexa App!

To access the **Now Playing** page on your tablet or mobile phone, when you have media playing you need to then tap on the Player, which loads on the bottom of whatever page you're viewing (the Player is always visible on every page of the mobile App when media plays).

To access the **Now Playing** page on your PC or Mac, simply click on the option from the Menu.

Whichever way you get to the **Now Playing** page, the same options will be offered, but in slightly different, not particularly significant, layouts.

For much of your audio content, the **Now Playing** page displays an image of the media playing – for example an album cover image – plus an icon for the source such as iHeartRadio, Kindle audiobooks or a podcast on TuneIn to remind you where the media is coming from. Under those images, is the media *Player*.

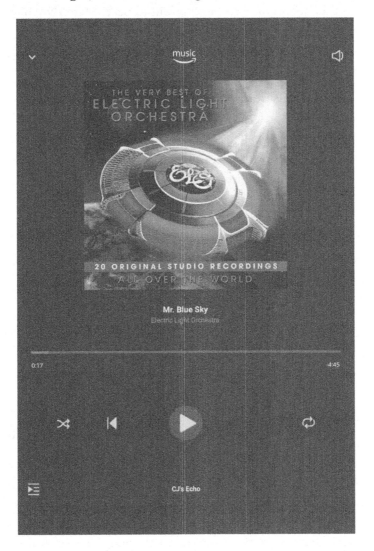

You can manually click any option on the *Now Playing* page or you can use voice. The *Player* always offers these control symbols:

- **Play/Pause:** Manually select or say, "Pause," "Resume," "Play" or "Stop."
- **Go back:** Manually select or say, "Go back."

- **Go forward:** Manually select or say, "Go forward."

- **Sound level slide:** If you don't see this slide immediately, click on the Loudspeaker icon and it will appear. Slide the volume bar manually or use a verbal command such as "volume seven" or "mute." Note that on your tablet or mobile phone, the Loudspeaker icon may be at the top right of the *Now Playing* page.

- **Song progress bar:** When using the App on a computer, selecting a place earlier or later in the song isn't possible. Ability to change the place in the song varies on mobile devices. Another option is to use an Alexa-enabled device's touch screen to drag the song location back or forth.

Depending on what type of audio you are playing, additional options are shown on the player:

- **Thumb Up & Thumb Down:** Rate the media you're listening to, and Alexa will use your opinion to tailor your audio stations to your preferences.

- **Shuffle:** Selecting the crossed arrows will cause the Queue to be played in random order.

- **Repeat:** Select the looping arrows to repeat the song or station when it is completed.

Also visible on the *Now Playing* page on a PC or Mac, are two lists you can view, *Queue* and *History* by selecting your choice.

Queue: This is the list of selections in the media you've chosen, such as the Classical Focus Prime Station I'm currently enjoying. Expand your options for each piece by selecting the V-shaped symbol known as a caret. Note that you may not get all of these options each time – the options you get depends on the media source. Possible Queue options are:

- Add the song to your Library (we will go into much more detail about your music library in Chapter 5).

- Shop the Digital Music Store, which will open in a new page in the Digital Store with the standard features seen on all Amazon product pages.

- View album in Prime Music, if applicable, which will open in a page that looks very much like the Digital Store page but with the opportunity to buy any/all the songs on the recording.

- When listening to podcasts or radio stations, clicking the caret and expanding the box allows you to mark what your listening to as a Favorite program.

History: This is the list of media you've played from all sources.

Play anything from Queue or History by clicking it. Your choice will then become the audio content that on the *Now Playing* page.

When viewing the *Now Playing* page on a tablet or mobile phone, you will see an icon with 4 lines and a triangle; tap on this to access the *Queue* (if there is one), where you can then change what you're listening to if you wish. Other options as discussed above are more limited, or in fact not available, on the mobile version of the App.

Note that if you want to see your media *History* on a tablet or mobile, then select the Play icon at the bottom of the page (the circle with a triangle inside) and the top of the page will show your most recently played media.

CJ's Tips: Note that if you are playing a station and then select another media, the station might be canceled. I learned this by pausing a station and asking for my news *Flash Briefing* (explained later but found in *Settings* if you want to explore it before we get to it). The station did not resume, even at my request. Stations are not canceled if you ask for your weather forecast, something from Wikipedia or a simple question. The station volume is reduced while Alexa fulfills the request. I'm still learning which requests cancel stations and which don't. If a station gets canceled, and I want to continue listening, it's right there in *History* where I can pick up where I left off.

Now Playing on Alexa-enabled devices with Screens

Most media will appear on the screen too, but the Player control options might be more limited. Tap the screen to see the Player, and tap the appropriate control to pause, play, go back or forward one song, drag the song to the end, shuffle the songs or repeat.

As mentioned above, if any of this is confusing right now then read on and return to this chapter once you have started playing some audio.

4: Watch This and More! — Video

For any voice command you read in this chapter be sure to use your wake word ("Alexa", "Amazon", etc) first.

If you have an Alexa device that does not have a screen, such as the Echo Show, you might feel this section is irrelevant to you, but it's worth reviewing what video services are currently available via the Alexa App and how to access them as some of them can, in fact, be used on your home TV set and controlled via Alexa with your voice.

Before we discuss all the Video options, please note that during the writing of this book, there was a major update to the Alexa App the result of which is that the Video section is a little harder to find on the App when viewed via a tablet or mobile phone. This situation may well change with the next update.

The best way to get to it is via **Settings > Alexa Preferences > TV & Video**.

In a minute we will look more closely at the Video services currently available. But before we do that, it's important to understand that there are two types of Video services for Alexa devices.

The first is what I call direct access, meaning that if you have an account with these services you can watch their content directly on an Echo Show. This is the case for Amazon Video and Prime Video, IMDB movie trailers, Hulu and NBC.

The second is best termed as indirect access; this is where you use your Alexa voice commands via the Echo Show (or any other connected Alexa-enabled device) to control the content streamed to your home television set from streaming or cable services such as Fire TV or Dish TV.

So, let's take the direct access services first.

Direct Access: Amazon Video and Prime Video

Amazon have two different ways in which you can access their vast library of digital content of TV shows and movies.

- **Amazon Video/ Rent or Buy:** In the first instance you can search in the section labeled Movies, Music and Games on Amazon. com, where you will find titles that can either be rented or bought outright; you'll also see titles that - as well as being available rent or buy - can also be accessed for "free" with a Prime Membership in the Prime Video. When you buy or rent content from Amazon it will appear in your Video Library.

- **Prime Video:** On the Amazon.com menu click on Prime Video to browse the thousands of movies and TV shows that are available at no additional cost with a Prime membership. Note that there are some movies and TV shows that are exclusive to Prime Video (known as Prime Originals); that is, you will need a Prime Membership to access them. Currently Amazon are offering the first month of membership for free, and then there are three membership options:

  - a simple Prime Video option for $8.99 per month.

  - an all-inclusive Prime Monthly option at $12.99 per month which includes free delivery, unlimited music streaming via Prime Music, plus unlimited Kindle books and photo storage.

  - a Prime Annual membership option for $119 a year for the all-inclusive deal.

- **Prime Channels/ Subscription:** Amazon has also organized a number of link-ups with third-party TV channels – such as HBO, Showtime, PBS Kids - so that you can stream their content direct to your screen via your Prime membership. To be completely clear, you will first need to have a full Prime monthly membership, and then each Prime Channel has a further monthly fee (Showtime is currently being offered for $10.99 a month, whilst HBO is more expensive at $14.99 a month). To find out more about which

Channels are available, go to *Amazon.com* > *Prime Video* > *Prime Video Channels*.

Media available on the above options can be watched on any device with a screen including your personal computer, Amazon Fire devices, Echo Show and Echo Spot, iOS and Android devices, TVs and more.

Watch Amazon and Prime Video/ Prime Channels via Alexa: If you have a device that has both a screen and is Alexa-enabled, there are many ways you can access Amazon and Prime content.

- **Search your library:** Say "Show me my video library" or "Show me my Watch List," and it will appear on your screen where you can browse and select what you want to watch.

- **Search by title:** Say "Show me [specific movie or show title]", and it will play.

- **Show by actor or genre:** Say, "Show me Harrison Ford movies," or "Show me animated movies," and search results you can browse will appear on the screen.

Alexa will reply, "Here's what I found," to all these requests as the results appear.

Once the content is being shown, you can control it two ways:

- Tap or click on the screen to view and use the Player that includes pause/play and symbols for going back or forward 10 seconds.

- Use voice with common commands including: "Play/ pause/ resume", "Rewind/ fast forward", "Go back/ skip ahead and number of seconds, minutes or hours", "Next video/ next episode".

Direct Access: Movie Trailers from IMDB

You can watch any move trailer from IMDB by simply asking Alexa. Say, "Show me the movie trailer for [movie title]."

As before you can control the trailer playback either manually or using voice control.

CJ's Tips: I quite like using my Echo Spot to watch movie trailers, they are exactly the kind of short video content that work really well on the small screen. I'm not convinced there's much value in being able to play the rest of my Video Library on a small screen such as the Spot, as I'd far prefer to view most TV series and movies on a bigger screen like my TV.

Direct Access: Watch Roku Hulu and NBC on Echo Show

To enjoy these services on your Echo Show you first need to have a subscription with either Roku, Hulu or, in the case of NBC, a cable subscription and an NBC profile.

Then in the Alexa App you select Settings > Alexa Preferences > TV & Video and then follow the prompts to link the service you want to the service to Alexa. After that, simply ask Alexa to "Play _____ on Hulu" or "Show _____ on NBC".

These new options are particularly useful if you already have a Roku, Hulu or NBC (cable) subscription. Both services offer interesting content, TV series and shows, with Hulu having the slight edge of also offering live sports events and essentially offering you a link up with several different TV channels including NBC, ABC, HGTV, the Disney channel and more.

If you don't already have a subscription to these services, you can find out more about the various plans on www.roku.com, www.hulu.com or for access to NBC, contact your local cable provider (note that you need to also create and NBC profile via the www.nbc.com website.)

Direct Access: Netflix on Echo Show

This new, and much anticipated, partnership has only just been announced for the All-New Echo Show 10 (3rd Generation) launch at the end of 2020; the information from Amazon is unclear as to whether you'll also be able to access Netflix on the smaller or previous generation Echo Shows.

However, on the Echo Show 5 and 8 you can already ask Alexa to "Open Silk" or "Open Firefox" browsers and a mobile version will appear on your Echo Show screen; and then you can login to your Netflix account.

Further, if you own a smart TV that supports version 5.3.0 of the Netflix app, then you can also upload the Alexa App onto your TV.

You can then pair your Echo Show to the App on your smart TV and use your Show as a speaker to send voice commands to your TV and thus navigate Netflix by saying, for example, "Play Stranger Things on Netflix" and so on.

Indirect Access: Fire TV

The original Fire TV dongle from Amazon is a comprehensive media streaming device. It can be installed and used entirely independently, with or without its own Alexa-enabled remote control. Or, it can also be paired with and controlled by other Alexa-enabled devices, such as the Amazon Echo.

The same is true for the Toshiba Fire TV edition television set – a smart TV that has Fire TV streaming already integrated and which can be voice-controlled when you pair it to the Alexa-enable remote or to one of your other Alexa-enable devices.

Furthermore, there is now also the Fire TV Cube which already has Alexa preinstalled, ready to operate with voice control alone.

What you can watch with Fire TV: Most streaming and live TV services can be viewed with Fire TV including: Netflix, Hulu, HBO Now, Crackle, Amazon, ESPN, Showtime, Sling, DirectTV Now, NBA, MLB. TV, CNN, Comedy Central, HGTV and AMC.

What else you can do with Fire TV and Alexa: Enjoy music services played through your equipment such as Amazon Music, and iHeartRadio, order pizza or an Uber, browse Yelp and play games from developers like EA and Disney. Search "Fire TV" on Amazon.com to see everything the service offers.

Connecting Alexa and Fire TV: Amazon provides complete instructions for setting up Fire TV equipment and a PDF Users Guide to make the most of Fire TV. To control Fire TV with Alexa:

• Go to *Settings* > *Alexa Preferences* > *TV & Video* in the Alexa App and select *Fire TV*.

• Select *Link Your Alexa Device*.

• Select the device you want to link.

• Follow the onscreen prompts to complete linking of Alexa to the Fire TV Player.

Once setup is complete, put Alexa to work with requests like:

• "Watch Game of Thrones"

• "Next episode"

• "Rewind 10 minutes"

• "Jump to 30 minutes"

• "Show me Emma Watson movies"

• "Play Sia music"

• "Order Domino's pizza"

And literally thousands of other requests. To be clear, linking your Alexa-enabled device will allow you to control your Fire TV options on your TV, and will only work to watch Fire TV content on your television screen if you have one of the Fire TV devices.

Indirect Access: Dish TV

This service appeals mostly to those that already have a Dish TV package (www.dish.com/programming/packages), which currently starts at $59.99/month and includes the Hopper DVR. Dish TV pushes its Alexa relationship by periodically offering new customers an Echo Device upon signup. You can check the availability of this offer at www.dish.com.

To be clear, to control Dish TV via Alexa you will need a Dish TV Package and the DISH Hopper Smart DVR (the Hopper 3 and newer, Hopper with Sling, Hopper and Wally are all currently supported.)

Connecting Dish TV to Alexa:

- Go to *Settings* > *Alexa Preferences* > *TV & Video* in the Alexa App and select *Dish TV*.

- Enable the Skill.

- Have your Dish TV and Amazon login information handy, since you might need to enter it during setup. Follow the instructions to connect Alexa to Dish TV which include 1.) turning on your Hopper DVR box and TV 2.) Enter the code given on the TV screen into the Alexa App.

- You might need to update your Hopper's software to the latest version before you can use Dish TV with Alexa. On your Dish set-top box, navigate to channel 9607 and locate/select "software update" to update your receiver to the latest software. Allow the software update to complete and the Hopper box to restart before returning to the Alexa app to attempt to link again.

- Select *Finish Setup* in the Alexa App.

- Follow on-screen prompts to link to the TV or other equipment you use to watch TV and other video services.

If you have issues with the process, try these fixes:

Update the Alexa App, and make sure you signed into the App with the same account information you used to register your Alexa-enabled device - that is, make sure your app and device are on the same account. Double-check to make sure you've enabled the Alexa Video Skill for Dish TV (or another video provider you're setting up). And failing all of that, contact Dish TV directly.

Once setup is complete you can ask Alexa to control your Dish TV viewing by saying things like:

- "Go to channel 75"

- "Find Modern Family on Dish" — Alexa will look for options on the services you have such as Netflix, Hulu and Amazon Prime)

- Play your recorded content ("Play Dallas Cowboys football game")

- Pause, fast-forward and rewind what's being shown ("Rewind 2 minutes")

Other TV Service Providers

Note we have only mentioned the bigger TV service providers above, but over the years other – perhaps less well-known – service providers have also developed Alexa Skills. Just as for Dish TV, you can enable these Skills on the Alexa App and then ask Alexa to control those services via voice-command. A complete and ever-changing list of TV service providers that have Alexa compatible Skills can be found at **Settings > Alexa Preferences > TV & Video**.

A Word about YouTube

Back in October 2017 Google, the owners of YouTube, removed access to YouTube videos on the original Echo Show. There used to be a clever, but slightly boring, work around to get YouTube regardless, but now, with the 2nd Generation Echo Show there is an even easier and better work around!

Basically, Amazon have added browser support in the new Echo Show 2nd Generation – with currently the Silk and Firefox bowsers available. To open a browser, simple say "Open Silk" or "Open Firefox" and a mobile version will appear on your Echo Show screen. From there you can manually type in the YouTube address and then bookmark it for future use! Simple!

You can also use the browser in this way to access your Netflix account on the Echo Show!

5: Songs by the Millions — Music

For any voice command you read in this chapter be sure to use your wake word ("Alexa", "Amazon", etc) first.

It's difficult to beat Alexa for the ease and convenience of playing music from a diverse range of sources. But working out how to find and set up these different sources is not always that obvious!

For a start, setting up music services via the Alexa App on a PC or Mac is not ideal since not all services are compatible with the browser version of the App! That is why I recommend that you set up your Alexa music services from the Alexa App on a tablet or mobile phone.

To be clear, Alexa doesn't have access to any music on her own.

So you will not be able to play any music via your Alexa-enabled device until you have linked Alexa to your music provider of choice. Naturally, there are lots of options! We'll cover the main ones below (Amazon Music, Spotify, TuneIn, Apple Music and so on) but, as there are constant updates to this part of the App, it pays to check in from time to time to see if there are any new options that you like.

Navigating the Entertainment Page

On the App on your tablet or a mobile phone you'll see at the bottom a round icon with a triangle inside, the Play icon, which takes you to the *Entertainment* page.

On this page you will see any Amazon Music, Podcasts, Audible and Kindle eBooks that you already own and have recently played/ viewed.

This area will be blank if you haven't used any of those media yet. For example, when I first started my Alexa App on my tablet, I'd already downloaded some Kindle books to that tablet, so that's what I saw on the landing page; when I then set up an Audible and Amazon Prime Music account, I subsequently found my music and audio books listed here too.

Scrolling down towards the bottom you'll see suggestions of music services you can link to, for example Spotify, and a link called **Manage Your Services**.

Click on **Manage Your Services** and you'll see Settings to choose your **Default Services**, a **Profanity Filter** option and your existing music/ podcast services (if you have any) and the option to **Link New Services**, where you'll be able to follow prompts to link to the music services of your choice.

So now let's look at some of the music services you can connect to via Alexa in more detail:

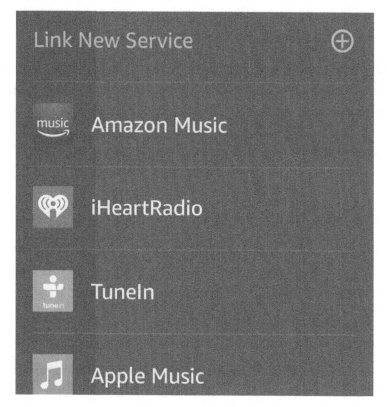

Amazon Music on the Alexa App

Amazon have their own music service called Amazon Music. There are different options: Amazon Music or Amazon Music Unlimited, and further options if you are an Amazon Prime customer (see below). As well as the subscriptions services, you can also simply buy digital music from Amazon here: amzn.to/33oofT6

To be clear, **Amazon Music on the Alexa App** is where you access your personal music and/ or podcast collection that are either:

- Available as part of the free Amazon Music option.

- OR from a paid Prime Music OR Amazon Music Unlimited subscription.

- And/or any digital music or audio content that you have bought on Amazon outside of the subscription services.

Linking Amazon Music to Alexa: select *Amazon Music* from either the *Entertainment* landing page or the *Manage Your Services* page; then open and install the Amazon Music app to your mobile device.

Explore the Amazon Music app to create all the different playlists, music preferences you want (see more on this below).

The Amazon Music app will then effectively communicate your choices to the Alexa App; you can also choose options to upgrade from the free Amazon Music account to the Amazon Music Unlimited account here.

CJ's Tips: The Amazon Music app for your desktop computer is Amazon's equivalent of the iTunes app. Once you have it installed you can play all the music in you Amazon Music account on your PC or Mac just like you probably do on iTunes already.

Amazon Music vs Amazon Music Unlimited vs Prime Music

This is possibly one of the most confusing aspects of Amazon's many services, so don't be worried if it all seems unnecessarily complicated. It is. But here's the easiest way to think of it: Amazon Music is free and very good, Amazon Music Unlimited and Prime Music are not free and are very, very good!

Amazon Music Free: The basic Amazon Music offer is free and gives you access to selected top playlists, podcasts and thousands of music streaming stations BUT includes ads. There are also more limited features, for example you cannot create your own playlists.

Prime Music: This option is available as part of Amazon's standard monthly Prime membership deal, to be clear, you need to have the Prime membership deal to benefit.

- Benefits: stream 2 million songs in Prime Music, create your own playlists, and a long list of other Prime shipping, shopping and media benefits that can be viewed on Amazon.

- Standard annual: $119/year, after 30-day free trial.

- Standard monthly: $12.99/month, after a 30-day free trial.

There is also a student plan for $6.49/month or $59/year; and a plan for those who qualify for an EBT or Medicaid card, $5.99/ month.

Amazon Music Unlimited: If music is your thing and you want the fullest access possible to every available track or album than an Amazon Music Unlimited subscription is probably your best choice.

- Unlimited access to 70 millions songs, plus all the features of the Amazon Music app.

- New members get the first three months free and then switch to a paid-for plan. Individual plans are currently $7.99/ month, whilst a family plan is $14.99/month which can be used by up to 6 members. Annual memberships both for individuals and families are also available.

- There is also a specific single device plan for use with an Amazon Echo or a Fire TV device for $3.99/ month. And a student plan for just $4.99/ month.

Amazon Music Unlimited HD: There is also this further HD service, launched in September 2019 to coincide with the arrival of the new high-fidelity smart speaker, Echo Studio.

This is a further tier of music provision from Amazon with over 70 million songs available in High Definition (HD) or Ultra High Definition (ultra HD). If you are a serious music buff, this is an option worth considering. New users get 90 days free and then switch to a paid-for plan. At the time of writing the payment options available were:

- Amazon Music Unlimited subscribers: an additional $5 per month (Individual or Family plans only)

- Prime members: an additional $12.99 per month

- General Amazon customer (neither Prime members nor Amazon Music Unlimited subscriber): $14.99 per month

CJ's Tips: For what it's worth, my recommendation is getting a Prime membership since it offers so many other benefits, and if you then don't find enough of the kind of music you enjoy, consider adding a Music Unlimited subscription. Again, you can manage all music subscriptions from this here: www.amazon.com/music/settings

Search in Amazon Music and Amazon Music Unlimited

Once you've downloaded the Amazon Music app on your mobile device and linked it to Alexa, the easiest way to search for songs is simply to ask Alexa for them!

But you can also go into the Amazon Music app via the Alexa App and use the search box. As you type the search word, a list of results will begin to populate and gradually narrow the more of the term you complete.

Depending on whether or not you have the free or the Unlimited versions of Amazon Music, you'll be able to see numerous options like *Playlists/ Stations/ Artists/ Albums/ Songs/ Genres*. Using them is a very straightforward process, so just a few comments will suffice for each.

Playlists: In the free Amazon Music the most current popular playlists are shown here; in Unlimited you have much more of these curated playlists to choose from.

Amazon's Playlists are curated "albums" of music that have been put together by Amazon's team. Like the stations they are categorized according to genre or music era or artist, but in this case there will be a finite selection of tracks – for example 50 Great Feel-Good Classics. More than 1,700 Amazon Music Playlists have been curated, and the number is growing, so give yourself a day off to have a good look around!

Stations: Amazon's Stations are music streams based on either a particular artist, era of music, or genre of music. Theoretically, if you choose a Station – just like the radio in the olden days – you will get that type of music on an endless stream. This is a good way to search for music in line with your preferences.

CJ Tips: You can also explore all the options for your Amazon Music services on your PC or Mac at music.amazon.com

Search in Amazon Prime Music

Again, the easiest way to search for songs is simply to ask Alexa for them!

But if you have a Prime Music subscription, when you link to Amazon Music via the Alexa App and explore, your Prime Music options will be searchable here. If you click at the bottom where it says Find you can search for music either by *Genre, Stations, Playlists, Charts, New Releases* and so on, as explained above.

You can simply click on a Station or a Playlist shown to have Alexa play it; or when you know the title of the Playlist, you can just ask Alexa, for example: "Play 90s Dance Anthems". However, to avoid too much searching around, you might prefer to add the Prime Playlists that you like to your Library.

CJ Tips: In my experience, it helps to be as specific as possible when asking for music, such as, "Play Bruce Springsteen Born to Run from my Library," or "Play Bruce Springsteen Born to Run from Amazon Prime Music." Once you have a few different music services set up it helps Alexa if you let her know exactly which service you want the music to come from. I will talk about setting Default Music Services later to make this process even easier.

Add Amazon Unlimited and Prime Music Playlists to your Library

There are two ways to add Playlists:

Manually via the Alexa App:

First go to the Amazon Music app via the Alexa App (***Play icon > Entertainment landing page > Amazon Music > Open App***) and find a Playlist you like, start it playing and then tap the + ***sign***. It will be automatically added to your library.

By Voice via the Alexa App:

First go to the Amazon Music app via the Alexa App (***Play icon > Entertainment landing page > Amazon Music > Open App***) and find a Playlist you like, start it playing and then simply ask to "add this playlist to my library" and Alexa will do just that!

CJ's Tips: Every track you hear on a Prime Playlist or Station comes from an album that is also available for you to listen to free as a Prime member. However, adding an album to your Music Library may require a little bit of detective work.

Here's an example... you hear the song "Don't" by Ed Sheeran on a Prime Playlist and decide you would like to listen to the whole album that the song comes from.

- First go online to Amazon Prime Music by going to music.amazon. com in the browser of your desktop computer.

- Second search "Don't Ed Sheerin" in the search box at the top of the page and hit enter.

- Third, your results will be shown so scroll down to Prime Songs and when you see the song "Don't, Ed Sheeran" click the three vertical dots to the right of the track. A pop-up window will appear giving you further options and one of those options should be *View Album*.

- Fourth, go ahead and click *View Album* and you will be shown the entire album that the track is from plus the option to + *Add to My Music*, and clicking that will add the album (in this example the album is called "X (Wembley Edition)") to your music library.

Now you're all set and can just ask "Alexa, play the album X from my Music Library"

Spotify

With 232 million users and 108 million subscribers, www.spotify.com is one of the largest music streaming platforms. While Spotify has a free subscription, a premium account is required for use with Alexa. That's Spotify's choice. The current cost of a premium account is $9.99/month for those who have not tried Premium before. Besides using their service with the Alexa devices, benefits include the ability to download music to your devices to listen offline, skip songs you don't like as often as you want, play any song and listen without ads.

To create an account, choose an email address to link to, a password, user name and payment method, which can be a credit card or PayPal. If you choose PayPal, Spotify will connect to PayPal, and you might have to sign in. Once on PayPal, you will select which payment associated with your account you want to use.

Linking Spotify to Alexa: Once you have a premium account, select Spotify from the *Play icon > Entertainment > Manage Your Services* page, and choose *Link your account > Authorize the*

Account (if asked).

A new window will open where you will have to authorize the connection of Alexa to your Spotify account. Once you do that, return to the Alexa App where you will be asked whether you want to make Spotify your default music service. If you want to change that later, it can be done at *SSettings* > *Music & Podcasts* > *Default Services*. There, you can select a Default music library and a Default station service.

If you want to unlink your Spotify account, select *Settings* > *Music & Podcasts* > *Spotify* and *Unlink Account* from Alexa. On that page, you can also go to Spotify to Manage Spotify Settings such as upgrade to a Premium for Family account, view and edit your profile or see when the next Renew date is.

Using Spotify with Alexa: If you've made Spotify your Default music service, you can use your voice or the Spotify app to play music from the service. For voice, simply request music from your favorite artist, and Alexa will play it. If it's not the Default service, you'll have to say, "Play Selena Gomez on Spotify," for example. As usual, the *Player* will appear on the *Now Playing* page and at the bottom of any other page you're viewing. Manually control Player functions using the Alexa App or via a screen on Alexa-enabled devices that have one, or more simply, with your voice.

Pandora

Pandora is often referred to as an online radio pioneer, having been launched at the dawn of Internet radio streaming services back in 2000. Currently Pandora is only available in the USA. But it's popularity is as good as ever, with over 160 million users, and over 30 million tracks available, it's safe to say that Pandora will be here for a while longer.

One of the benefits of Pandora, for our purposes, is that you can use Alexa with a free Pandora account, which I do. If you already have an account, you can skip to *Linking Alexa to Pandora* below.

There are currently three membership levels, see www.pandora.com:

- **Pandora Free:** Free; Ad-supported radio; Personalized stations

- **Pandora Plus:** $4.99/month; 30-day free trial; Ad-free Personalized stations; Better audio; Offline radio

- **Pandora Premium:** $9.99/month; 60-day free trial; Ad-free; Create new stations and playlists rather than personalizing existing stations; Better audio; No limit on skips and replays; Download music to other devices

Select the level you prefer, and you'll be taken to an account signup page. Even if you select a free trial for a paid subscription, providing an email address and password on the first page will immediately begin a free account.

Linking Pandora to Alexa: Back on the Alexa App, select Pandora from the *Play icon* > *Entertainment* > *Manage Your Services* page. Then, choose *Link your account* > *Authorize the link*.

Using Pandora with Alexa: Once Alexa and Pandora are linked, you'll have two options on the Pandora page on the Alexa App.

- Choose + *Create Station*, and enter an artist, genre or track to search or scroll through the *Browse Genre* section to view more than 60 genres from standards like Rock, Alternative, Classical, Hip Hop/Rap, Instrumental, Comedy and Decades to niche categories like Game Day, Mexico, Rainy Day, Pandora Local and Driving.

- Browse and choose one of the stations listed below *My Stations*, a list that will populate once you start adding stations or will be displayed immediately if you link to an existing account. Toggle Sort by date (date added) and Sort by A-Z to view the My Stations list. The first entry will always be Shuffle to mix the list randomly.

As usual, the *Player* will appear and at the bottom of the page and/or on the *Now Playing* page and can be used to control the music. Voice and screen controls (if relevant) work too.

CJ's Tips: I like Pandora, they have some great stations and I have no problem asking Alexa for a station based around an artist like, "Alexa, play Adele on Pandora," but things get more problematic when I ask for a themed playlist like "Alexa, play Laid Back Brunch on Pandora." There were many stations like this that got no response from Alexa even when I set Pandora as my default station service.

If you encounter this problem then the solution is simply to go to **entertainment > Pandora > Browse Genre** on the Alexa App and start a playlist playing. It will immediately be added as one of your stations and will appear under My Stations. Now try again to ask for it with your voice and you should have no problem.

iHeartRadio

This radio network and internet radio platform offers an immense amount of content including music and podcasts provided by 800 iHeartRadio partner stations in the US, more than 1,000 artist stations and a range of other media.

There are three membership levels:

- **iHeartRadio:** No cost, but you're limited to choosing a local radio station or curated stations built around well-known artists but including similar artists.

- **iHeartRadio Plus:** $4.99/month; Play any song on demand; Unlimited skips; Save songs to create a single playlist; Replay songs from live radio and custom stations.

- **iHeartRadio All Access:** $9.99; Everything offered in Plus; Unlimited access to millions of songs; Listen offline on iOS and Android versions; Create as many playlists as you like.

I tried All Access but settled on the free iHeartRadio account simply because I've got so many other music choices that I don't need a paid service. If you start out with a free account, select the Upgrade Now tab on iHeartRadio at any time to try one of the paid plans.

Linking iHeartRadio to Alexa: Select iHeartRadio from the **Play icon > Entertainment > Manage Your Services** page and then

Link Your Account. Authorize the link to an existing account or create a free or upgraded account with personal and payment information.

Using iHeartRadio with Alexa: The homepage has a search box where you can type in keywords including an artist's name, genre or city, for example. Searches return results related to your keyword, and they're divided into four categories:

- **Stations** — Artist Stations are titled after well-known artists to give you an idea of the flavor of the music, but each station includes songs from a range of artists. I'm currently listening to the station called Adele. The song Queue includes Rihanna, Ed Sheeran, Lorde, Ellie Goulding, OneRepublic and others in addition to Adele.

- **Songs** — Singles by title or group name related to the keyword.

- **Artists** — Bands, solo acts, choirs, etc. with names related to the keyword.

- **Talk Shows** — Shows and podcasts with names related to the keyword.

Your second option to locate music is the Browse section with three categories to look through:

- **Live Radio:** 800+ radio stations from around the country.

- **Shows:** These are mostly podcasts and the 20+ categories include Business & Finance, Comedy, Crime, Entertainment, Politics, Spirituality and Sports. Categories contain a dozen to more than 100 show options.

- **Favorites:** You have the option to select any station or show as a Favorite, and it will be saved here for easy locating later, though it might not show up immediately.

Manually select any Station or Show, and it will begin to play. When using voice, be as specific as possible for the most accurate results.

Once playing, the content can be controlled on the *Now Playing* page, via the player at the bottom of any other page or with your voice. Also on the *Now Playing* page, you have the option to expand any selection in the Queue to:

- Tune the Station by choosing what you want to play — Top Hits,

Mix or Variety. I don't know what the difference is between Mix and Variety, though perhaps seasoned iHeart enthusiasts will.

- Select the Station as a Favorite (check out my Tip below).

- Rate the song with thumb up or down symbols.

- Create new station around your favorite artists.

- Shop Digital Music Store on Amazon for material from the artist — a new window will open to Amazon.

CJ's Tips: Again, you need to be very exact when asking Alexa for something from iHeartRadio, especially when asking for a radio station. I find saying "Alexa, play 102.7 KIIS-FM Los Angeles" is a bit of a mouthful and can be hard to remember precisely. I prefer to save my radio stations as favorites via the Now Playing page and then I find that Alexa is much more likely to understand what I am requesting.

TuneIn

TuneIn is one of the oldest streaming services, founded in 2002. Today, its specialties are Music, News, Sports and Talk, and TuneIn carries local, national and international content. Free and Premium accounts are available:

- **TuneIn Radio:** Free; Ad-supported. Stream 100,000 radio stations covering the range of styles.

- **TuneIn Premium:** $9.99/month; Ad-free. Stream 100,000 radio stations, 600 ad-free music stations, audio books and podcasts; Listen to live coverage of sports events including play-by-play of every NFL, MLB, NBA, and NHL game and more.

- **TuneIn Live on Alexa:** This is a specific deal that was launched in March 2018 for customers who either have an Alexa-enabled device or an Amazon Prime membership. It is effectively an add-on to the Free TuneIn offer, and allows you to access the live coverage of sports events including play-by-play of every NFL, MLB, NBA, and NHL game and more. The price is currently $2.99/ month ($3.99/

per month for non-prime members that have an Alexa-enabled device). Note that this offer is mainly aimed at owners of Amazon's Echo products, and is not currently fully integrated with some third-party Alexa-enabled devices such as the Sonos One smart speaker.

Linking TuneIn to Alexa: On the ***Play icon* > *Entertainment* > *Manage Your Services*** page, select ***TuneIn* > *Link your account* > *Authorize the link*.** You can create an account there by providing the standard information, choosing the membership level you prefer and providing payment information if you choose Premium or Live on Alexa.

Using TuneIn with Alexa: The TuneIn homepage is set up much like the iHeartRadio page with a search box and more specific means of searching.

- Using the Search Box returns uncategorized results, unless you type in the exact name of the show or station you want, and that's a disadvantage compared with iHeartRadio. You're given a very long list of results to scroll through, and so I rarely use the function. Obviously, the more specific your search can be, the better results you'll get. You might have to try several searches using differing words or groups of words to find what you're looking for.

- The Browse function is more successful, and here TuneIn has the edge on iHeartRadio. Select from:

    — Favorites, which is empty at first but will be populated as you "Favorite" content you like.

    — Local Radio based on where you've given as your location at Settings > Your Echo Device > Device Location > Edit.

    — Trending list of stations and shows currently popular.

    — Music that is divided into 40+ subcategories for decade and musical genre.

    — Talk with 30+ genre subcategories.

    — Sports with 20+ subcategories including popular US, European and world sports, fantasy football and podcasts.

— News with a short list of trending shows from popular sources such as NPR, CNN and BBC, and two expandable subcategories: More Shows and Recent Episodes.

— By Location allows you to find news from continents and regions around the globe.

— By Language, with more than 90 languages offered.

— Podcasts broken into Music, Sports and Talk categories and subcategories.

Once you choose a **Category > Subcategory** from Search or Browse results, a list of shows will be displayed for you to select from. Using the App for this purpose, rather than voice, is the best method.

CJ's Tips: Even if you know what you want, Alexa might have difficulty with your request if you use voice. For example, I said, "Play ESPN Outside the Lines," a popular show. Alexa replied, "Do you want me to add an outside station to your Pandora account?" No, but thanks for asking. The request, "Outside the Lines, ESPN" had Alexa take me to a random ESPN station.

This again demonstrates that the more content available through Alexa, the more specific you'll need to be if using voice, and your request still might not produce the desired results. I use the app, and when I locate a station, show or podcast I want to return to, I "Favorite" it immediately, so I don't have to go searching for it later.

SiriusXM

SiriusXM started by offering satellite radio services and has expanded into a subscription based online radio where it's a good fit for Alexa. There are 70+ music channels, 20+ talk and entertainment channels, 10+ sports channels including live play-by-play of major sports events, leagues and college sports, 15+ news and issues channels, traffic and weather, Latin, Comedy and more.

Alexa's relationship with SiriusXM is different than it is with iHeartRadio, TuneIn, Spotify and Pandora. SiriusXM is an Alexa Skill, so the platform isn't supported to the same extent as the other services. We'll cover Alexa Skills in detail in a later chapter. It being a Skill might be why the Alexa & SiriusXM connection is more problematic. I suggest you read the information on the SiriusXM page on the Alexa App for an overview and for ratings from users.

The Sirius XM skill is currently rated just 2/5 stars, with many more negative reviews than positive ones. Problems include connecting with and accessing SiriusXM, Alexa not recognizing login information or saying it is wrong, and linking to SiriusXM causing user's Echo devices to stop working entirely. The last issue is especially concerning, though I haven't experienced it. My experience has been that Customer Service at Sirius isn't up to speed about linking Amazon Alexa with SiriusXM at this writing.

Here's something else that might deter you from opening a new SiriusXM account, and it is due to it being a Skill rather than a fully supported service: you can't search or browse SiriusXM from the Alexa App. Using voice is the only current option. You must know the name of what you want to hear or use trial and error to find what you want. I said, "Play football on SiriusXM." The first response was, "What do you want to hear?" When I asked again, the reply was, "I couldn't find a station called 'football' on SiriusXM."

Linking SiriusXM to Alexa: If you want to proceed and have a SiriusXM account:

- Scroll to **SiriusXM** on the *Play icon* > *Entertainment* > *Manage Your Services* page or search for the Skill in the *Skills* section of the Alexa App.

- Select *Enable* and follow the prompts. You will need to have your SiriusXM online login details available.

Apple Music

For Mac users a very welcome update to the latest music providers available via Alexa is, of course, Apple Music. In theory, the service allows you to stream over 70 million songs ad-free from Apple Music.

But like SiriusXM, the Apple Music service on Alexa is provided via a Skill that you need to Enable. As a result, users have found it a bit hit and miss in terms of getting the Skill to work, stay connected and being user friendly. I suspect these bugs will be ironed out as more and more users take advantage of this option.

Linking Apple Music to Alexa: on the Alexa App, select *Apple Music from the Play icon > Entertainment > Manage Your Services* page. Then, choose Apple Music and then Enable.

You will need an active Apple Music subscription, so have your Apple ID ready to input when prompted.

Deezer

Deezer is one of the new kids on the block in the US market, but has been around for quite a while in Europe having been created in 2006 in Paris. A cross between Spotify and TuneIn, Deezer is an internet-based music streaming service. The service currently boasts of having 53 million licensed titles in its library, with more than 30,000 stations 14 million active users per month and 6 million paying subscribers as of April 3, 2018.

To use Deezer with Alexa, you will need a Deezer Premium + account which costs $9.99 / month. Then, similar to SiriusXM, the Deezer service on Alexa is provided via the Deezer skill. So once you have registered your Deezer Premium + account on the Deezer website, you can then access the Alexa app and activate the Deezer skill (as you would for other Skills). When you do this, you will be prompted to link Alexa to your Deezer Premium account.

Other Music/ Radio Skills

It is worth noting that there are many other radio stations that are offering specific Skills on Alexa allowing you to connect directly to their online stream, from national sports coverage on CBS Sports to local radio stations such as Radio Milwaukee. If you have a favorite radio station it might be worth checking if it has an Alexa skill so you can enable it and enjoy via voice control. Go to Skills > Search all skills on the Alexa App to explore the possibilities.

Setting Default Music Service

I've mentioned Default Music Services a couple of times now so let's discuss them more fully. To find this option go to **Settings > Alexa Preferences > Music & Podcasts > Default Services.**

Whichever way you get there, you'll see your current options (they may change) include setting a default music library and a default station service.

Once a default has been chosen Alexa will always search that service first when you make a request like "Alexa, play Avril Lavigne". Choose your preferred library and station service based on which sources you use the most, and remember that if you want music from a different source you will have to state that resource in your request, for example, "Alexa, play Avril Lavigne from iHeartRadio".

One quirk to watch out for, I have Amazon Prime Music set as my default library and station service, but if I want to hear something from my Library I still have to specify it in my request and be really specific if I want a particular album. Example I asked Alexa "Play Earth, Wind & Fire" and, instead of tracks by the band Earth, Wind & Fire, Alexa started playing a track called "Earth, Wind and Fire" by Miguel from Prime Music. I tried again "Alexa, play Earth, Wind & Fire from my Library" and things got better as Alexa played a range of the band's tracks from across my Library, but I specifically wanted to hear the Greatest Hits album so I had to try once more, "Alexa, play Earth, Wind & Fire Greatest Hits" before I got exactly what I wanted

I just relay this fascinating anecdote to demonstrate that setting a default music service is still no substitute for getting into the habit of being as specific as possible with all your requests!

CJ's Tips: Once some music is playing via your Alexa-enabled device you can control it with your voice with some pretty obvious commands like "What's this song", "Pause", "Turn down the volume", "Resume", "Next song", "Repeat this song" etc.

But did you know you can be a bit more adventurous than that? Try asking "Play dinner party music" or "Play music I can dance to" and see what Alexa comes up with!

Setting Profanity Filter

To find this option go to **Settings** > **Alexa Preferences** > **Music & Podcasts** > **Profanity Filter**.

Setting Up Multi-Room Music

If, like me, you become such a fan of the Echo offerings that you end up having more than one Echo device in your home, you might want to set your devices up to play your music on all your devices throughout your home.

To be clear, this option allows you to hear the same music on two or more Echo devices at once. Also, ideally you'll be using Multi-Room with your Amazon Prime Music or Amazon Music Unlimited account; though you can also use it with streams from Spotify, Pandora, iHeartRadio, SiriusXM, and TuneIn.

Note that Multi-Room is not compatible with Bluetooth, and it will not work for audiobooks.

The setup is the same as creating a Group (discussed further in the Smart Home chapter) – in fact what you'll be doing is setting up a Group just for music. The best way to do this is via the Alexa App on your mobile phone or tablet. Here's what to do:

• Tap on the Devices icon (the little house with the two switches)

• Next tap the + **plus sign** at the top right corner and select Set Up Multi-Room Music

- The App will list all devices with speakers that are compatible; choose the devices that you want to be part of the Group, and click on **Save**.

When you're ready to use Multi-Room then all you have to do is say "Play [music selection] on [group name]" or "Play [radio station name]" on Pandora on [group name]".

Note that you can control the music from any Echo device that is part of the group

6: Read or Listen...or Both — Books

For any voice command you read in this chapter be sure to use your wake word ("Alexa", "Amazon", etc) first.

I must admit that I was not really that keen on the idea of audiobooks (though I do love reading), but actually trying out the option on my Echo Spot whilst relaxing before bed has been something of a revelation, and one that I enjoy exploring more and more. Here's how you too can listen to a vast library of written material using your Alexa-enabled device:

Audible

Audible is an Amazon company, and its offerings have been significantly expanded in the last few years from just audiobooks to podcasts and original content that sounds more like a radio drama than a book because it is written for voice and read by a cast. For example, the X-Files: Cold Cases audiobook is four hours of material adapted from the series and read by David Duchovny, Gillian Anderson and other original and new actors. Audible books are read in the original reader's voice, not Alexa's.

Currently, Audible boasts over 425,000 titles in their English language catalogue ranging across a wide selection of genres, so there is plenty to choose from!

At the time of writing, the standard gold monthly Audible plan includes:

- 30-day Free Audible trial with two Audible Originals and one free audiobook to keep (Audible Originals are exclusive titles that produced in the Audible studios).

- $14.95/month after, with the option to cancel at any time.

- 3 books per month – one standard audiobook and two Audible

Originals - and all books chosen during your subscription are yours to keep forever even if you cancel.

- 30% discount off additional audiobooks.

- If you don't like a book, you have an exchange period for trading it for another.

- Free Audible app that allows you to listen on all your devices.

- Whispersync syncing that keeps your place in an audiobook even when you switch devices.

Getting Started with Audible: Here's how to get started with your Audible account

- Sign up for a free trial at www.audible.com

- Sign into your Amazon account.

- Choose *Existing Payment Method* (which will be indicated with its last 4 digits) or choose *Add New Payment Method* and complete its details.

- Select *Start Your Membership*.

- Select your free book.

- Cancel within 30 days to avoid being charged, if desired.

Connecting Audible to Alexa: Once your Audible account is established and you've chosen some books, it's time to integrate Alexa with Audible:

- In the Alexa App on a PC or Mac: select Music, Video & Books > Audible. The audio books that you have chosen/ purchased will be listed ready to enjoy.

- In the Alexa App on a tablet or mobile phone: select the *Play* icon to get to the *Entertainment* page. The audio book will simply show up in the Audible section on this page, ready to be played.

Here's how to enjoy your Audible audiobooks on your Alexa-enabled device:

- From the Audible section, select the title you want to hear using manual controls or voice.

- It will appear on your Alexa App Player (and on the screen if your device has one).

- Use the available touch control options, if desired.

- Say, "Read my Audible book," and Alexa will ask which book, or you can request it by title.

- For books in progress, say, "Resume my Audible book"

- Use voice for controls like "Pause", "Go Forward", "Go Back", "Go to Chapter 7", "Read Louder" and similar requests.

- You can also say things like, "Stop reading in 15 minutes" and "Set a 15-minute sleep timer" to have Alexa end reading when you want.

Kindle Books

Amazon's Kindle has been an innovate eBook reader since its introduction. Now you can also listen to Kindle books with Alexa - no Kindle needed. Kindle books are read in Alexa's voice.

You can purchase Kindle books individually or choose a Kindle Unlimited. Here's what's currently offered:

- 30-day free Kindle Unlimited trial.

- Kindle Unlimited is $9.99/month and includes unlimited reading of 1 million book titles (new and recent books are not included) and magazines; note that not all of these million books are available to be listened to as audiobooks!

- Kindle books can also be borrowed, lent and rented. To find out more about these features visit https://amzn.to/2ytsbid

- With an Amazon Prime membership, you can select one Kindle First early release book and borrow one additional book free each month.

Getting Started with Kindle Books: Here's how to create a Kindle account:

- If you love eBooks, consider a Kindle Unlimited 30-day trial, and the books can be read on a Kindle reader or Kindle for PC.

- To start a free trial, sign into your Amazon account from the Kindle Unlimited page (https://amzn.to/2Of906h).

- Choose **Existing Payment Method** (which will be indicated with its last 4 digits) or choose **Add New Payment Method** and complete its details, then select **Start Your Membership**.

- Cancel within 30 days to avoid being charged, if desired.

- If you don't want Kindle Unlimited, purchase, borrow, rent or select free Kindle books.

- If you already have a Kindle account, the books Alexa can read will show up in the Kindle section of the Alexa App.

Connecting Kindle Books to Alexa: Once you have some Kindle Books in your Kindle account here's how to integrate Alexa with Kindle:

- **In the Alexa App on a PC or Mac:** select **Music, Video & Books > Kindle Books**. The Kindle books that you have chosen/ purchased will be listed ready to enjoy.

- **In the Alexa App on a tablet or mobile phone:** select the **Play** icon to get to the **Entertainment** page. Your book will simply show up in the Kindle Books section of on this page, ready to be played.

Listening to Kindle Books via Alexa: Here's how to enjoy your Kindle audiobooks on your Alexa-enabled device:

- From the Kindle section, select the title you want to hear or use your voice to request it hands-free.

- The book will appear on your Alexa App Player (and your device's screen, if it has one).

- Use the available touch control options, if desired, including selecting the chapter you want from the Player Queue.

- Use voice for controls like "Pause", "Go Forward", "Go Back", "Go to Chapter 7", "Read Louder" and similar requests.

- You can also say things like, "Stop reading in 15 minutes" and "Set a 15-minute sleep timer" to have Alexa end reading when you want.

CJ's Tips: Selected books in the Audible and Kindle services can be listened to and read at the same time, something Amazon calls "Immersion Reading." Not only is the text in front of you on your phone or reader, but it is narrated and highlighted too. Amazon says this feature, "sparks an extra connection that boosts engagement, comprehension, and retention, taking you deeper into the book." Most people either love it or can't tolerate it, so if you want to give it a try, learn more at www.audible.com/mt/Immersion.

Now that we've gone through all your audio entertainment options you might want to return to Chapter 3 about the *Now Playing* page to familiarize yourself with what that page of the Alexa App offers.

7: Write it Down & Get it Done — Lists

For any voice command you read in this chapter be sure to use your wake word ("Alexa", "Amazon", etc) first.

Alexa offers convenience you'll enjoy when making a Shopping List or To-do List. Both functions are explained in detail below.

To begin, choose the Lists tab from the app Menu to see both Shopping and To-do headings. You will see three options, at the top the words Create Lists (more about that later) and then Shopping and To-Do.

Shopping Lists

Creating and managing a shopping list to take with you on your mobile app or to print is convenient, and you might find the process fun too, as I do. Here are your options:

Adding items on your Shopping List

Voice: For just one item say, "Add walnuts to the shopping list" regardless of the page showing on the Alexa App. Currently, Alexa seems only able to deal with adding one item at a time, so if you have more than one item for your list, then this series of commands works best: first say, "Add items to my shopping list" and Alexa will say "OK, what shall I add?", say, "Walnuts" (without the Wake Word), then Alexa will say, "I've added walnuts to your shopping list, anything else?", say the next item and the back and forth dialogue will continue until, when Alexa next says "...anything else?", you say "No".

Manually: On the Alexa App via your tablet or mobile phone select Shopping List from the Lists page, then just tap on the blue text Add

Item or + sign, then types the item you want and tap enter.

On your PC or Mac, the interface of the **Shopping List** is not quite so streamlined; but still pretty easy to navigate. Once you've selected **Shopping Lis**t from the Lists page, type things you want to buy into the **Add Item** + box at the top of the page, and select the + **sign** or tap/ hit enter.

Managing items on your Shopping List: Whether inputted manually or by voice, the items will appear in the list with the most recent item at the top:

Voice: Say "What's on my shopping list," and Alexa will read the list out to you. Then say, "Remove brown rice from my shopping list" or "Remove item number 7 from my shopping list" to take it off the list. Saying "Check off" instead of "Remove" works too. When you next check your list on the App, the removed items will be checked off and in the completed section of the list. Note that you will need to access the list manually via your PC or tablet etc, to actually fully delete the item from the list.

Manually: On your tablet or mobile phone, swipe right to check off an item. It will then move automatically to the completed section of the list. Once in the completed section of the list you can then swipe left to either **Delete** the item off the list or **Restore** the item to the active shopping list. You can also just swipe left straight away to **Delete** the item, or to search for the item on Amazon.

On your PC or Mac, check off a purchased or unwanted item by selecting the box to its left, and a ✔ will appear in the box, the item will be ~~crossed out~~, and the **delete** option will appear on the right. Select the **Delete** option at right, if you want to remove it from the list, or leave it there as a reminder you've bought the item.

Once you go away from the list and return, checked items you haven't deleted will be moved to the **Completed** list where they can be viewed or deleted individually or all at once.

You can also either click on an item, or on the expand symbol (the "v") on the right to see options for searching for the item on Amazon or Bing, and to delete it. Viewing your list on a PC or Mac gives you an added advantage of being able to print items, just click on the **Print** option at the top of the list.

Other Functions on the Shopping List

Hear your Shopping List: I say, "Shopping list" to hear it because efficiency appeals to me. If you're more conversational, say "What's on my shopping list," or anything similar. The Alexa voice recognition technology has its voice-recognition "ears" open for "shopping list" almost regardless of what else you say. Try it!

View your Shopping List Active and Completed on the App: On a mobile device or tablet, when you check off an item it instantly appears underneath the "active" list under a heading title Completed; as mentioned before you can then swipe left to either delete or restore the item to your list.

On your PC or Mac, if you go away from your list and then come back to it, the checked items can be accessed via the link that says Completed at the bottom of the active list. You can then uncheck them to have them return to the active list, or delete them if you prefer. Note that you might have to click away from Lists and then go back into the Shopping List to see the items restored to the active list

CJ's Tips: On certain Alexa-enabled devices with screens, such as the Echo Show, you can also manage items on your lists by swiping left or right. Plus, any time you use voice to manage your list, the list will appear on the screen for about 30 seconds. You can also make the list appear by asking Alexa to "show my shopping list/ to-do list"

To-do Lists

The **To-do List** functions pretty much the same as the **Shopping List**. There are just a few differences when creating and managing this list compared to the Shopping List.

Adding items on your To-do List

Voice: Simply say, "Add call doctor to the to-do list" regardless of the page showing on the Alexa App. Alternatively, say "Add item to my to-do list" and Alexa will say "OK, what can I add for you?" or something similar, then say "Call doctor" (without the Wake Word), and Alexa will confirm that she's done it. Currently, Alexa seems only able to deal with adding one item at a time to the To-do list; and unlike the Shopping List, there is no way of creating a dialogue series for adding more items to the list.

Manually: On the Alexa App via your tablet or mobile phone select **To-do List** from the Lists page, then just tap on the blue text **Add Item** or **+ sign**, then type the item you want and tap enter.

On your PC or Mac, the interface of the **To-do List** is not quite so streamlined; but still pretty easy to navigate. Once you've selected **To-do List** from the Lists page, type things you want to do into the **Add Item** + box at the top of the page, and select the **+ sign** or tap/hit enter.

Managing items on your To-do List: Regardless of how inputted, the items will appear in the list with the most recent item at the top; and as with the Shopping List there are Active and Completed sections of the To-do List.

Voice: Say "What's on my to-do list," and Alexa will read the list out to you. Then say, "Remove call doctor from my to-do list". When you next check your list on the App, the removed items will be checked off and in the completed section of the list. Note that you will need to access the list manually via your PC or tablet to actually fully delete the item from the list.

Manually: On your tablet or mobile phone, swipe right to check off an item. It will then move automatically to the completed section of the list. Once in the completed section of the list you can then swipe left to either **Delete** the item off the list or **Restore** the item to the active shopping list. As with the Shopping List, swiping left on an item in the Active list will give you the options of **Delete** and/ or **Search** options.

On your PC or Mac, check off an item by selecting the box to its left, and a ✔ will appear in the box, the item will be ~~crossed out~~, and the **delete** option will appear on the right. Select the **Delete** option at right, if you want to remove it from the list, or leave it there as a reminder you've bought the item. As with the **Shopping List**, click on the claret in the Active list or swiping left will also give you the options to **Delete**.

Create Your Own List

A recent update to the App now allows you to create your very own list! Once you land on the **Lists** page, you can manually add a title in the space where it says **Create List**, or you can use voice by asking Alexa to create a list! Alexa will ask you what you want to call the list, and then what you want to add... the list you create will work exactly the same way as the To-Do list. I found it to be a handy option for making a guest list for my kid's birthday party.

Deleting or Archiving a List

You might want to delete a list once you've no use for it. The only way to do this is via the App (you cannot use you voice). On your mobile device you can swipe left on the title of your list to either Edit the title, or Archive it. Once archived you can tap on View Archive at the bottom of the page and then in the Archive swipe left on your list again to either Restore the list or Delete it completely.

On your PC or Mac, when you first arrive on the *Lists* page, you will see the V expand icon on the right and when you click on that you will have the option to archive the list, then view the archive and choose the Restore or Delete options there

Once you go away from the list and return, checked items you haven't deleted will be moved to the *Completed* list where they can be viewed or deleted individually or all at once. Viewing your list on a PC or Mac gives you an added advantage of being able to print items, just click on the *Print* option at the top of the list.

CJ's Tips: When it comes to shopping lists I would say that the major failing is the clunky way that you have to create the dialogue series to add more than one item at a time to your list by voice. For example, I have one of my Echo devices perfectly placed in the kitchen and what I want to do is wander around and say "Alexa, add milk, bread, apples, ham and chicken to my shopping list" but that doesn't work. So it's great when I'm in the kitchen and remember one item I need to add but if I want to make a long list I'm better off adding it manually via the Alexa App on my PC.

As is the case when learning about any Echo device and Alexa talent, some casual practice should prove fun and entertaining when a dose of patience is included!

8: Never Forget, Always Be On Time — Reminders, Alarms & Timers

For any voice command you read in this chapter be sure to use your wake word ("Alexa", "Amazon", etc) first.

For me, Alexa and the Echo Dot shine as a personal assistant in these categories. While reminders and alarms are similar, let's look at them separately to learn the nuances of each. Note that in the App menu the page label is just **Reminders & Alarms**, but Timers live here too

Reminders

This is a quick, easy way to avoid forgetting something urgent or important. A friend of mine stops by to see her elderly father several times a week and sets Reminders for him for the following day or two. When she can't get there in person, she calls her dad and does it remotely with her father's phone on Speaker mode.

Reminders can be set and managed manually or with voice, though using voice is easier.

To set and manage Reminders with voice:

• Say "Remind me to call the mechanic at 1pm".

• If you forget to give a time, Alexa will ask for one, and if you say "1," Alexa will ask, "Is that 1:00 in the morning or afternoon?" or similar and Alexa will say, "Okay, I'll remind you at 1pm".

• If you specify time but not date, Alexa will set up the reminder for today, so be sure to give the day, such as "tomorrow" or "Wednesday" for days this week, or give a date such as October 6.

• Once set, if your Alexa-enabled device has a screen, the Reminder will also flash up on the screen.

• **To cancel a Reminder**, use the day and time rather than what you wanted to be reminded of, so say, "Cancel the reminder for 1pm today," and Alexa will ask for clarification if needed.

• **Note:** You cannot currently edit a Reminder using voice.

To set and manage Reminders manually:

• Go to the **Reminders & Alarms** page where tabs for Reminders, Alarms and Timers appear.

• Select **Reminders**.

• Select + **Add Reminder**, and a form will appear.

• Fill in the spaces for Remind me to..., Date and Time.

• Select which device you want the reminder to be given on.

• Select **Cancel** or **Save** as appropriate.

• Note that your reminders appear on the Reminder page in chronological order of when they will occur, not when created.

- Manage any Reminder by selecting it, and you'll be taken to a page where you can Edit it or Mark as Completed.

- If you select **Edit**, you'll be taken to a page where you can edit the Reminder by selecting any of the details or **Delete** the Reminder.

- On a PC or Mac, when editing a Reminder using the App on a computer, you must click away from the detail you edited, so that it is not highlighted, before the Save option becomes active. The Save option is always active when editing Reminders on a tablet or mobile phone.

To see and manage Reminders on an Alexa-enabled Device screen:

- Say, "Show my reminders" and the list will display on the screen.

- To cancel a Reminder, swipe it to the left, and it will disappear from the screen and the list in the App.

Getting your Reminders: With the default setting, Alexa gives a two-tone chime and says, "Here's your reminder: Call the mechanic." The sequence happens twice a few seconds apart unless you say "stop". On Alexa-enabled devices with screens, a message will also flash up "It's 1pm. Here's your reminder: ...." The Reminder will stay on the screen until you select Dismiss or take another action such as change the volume that causes the screen to display something different.

Completed Reminders: After a reminder has been issued, it will move to the Completed Reminders section where you can view them. You're not currently able to delete them from this list. They might jog your memory about whether you did something on the list, though being reminded of it is not a guarantee you followed through. For example, a completed reminder on this list doesn't mean a person remembered to take their medication or feed the dog!

Alarms

Alexa gives you a range of alarm options which we'll get to shortly, but first, here are the basics. Oddly, you currently cannot set an alarm manually, only using your voice, so let's begin there.

Setting and managing Alarms using voice:

- Say, "Set an alarm for 6am".

- Alexa says, "Alarm set for 6am" and this will also be displayed on a screen if your device has one.

- Say "Cancel the alarm for 6am," and Alexa will say, "6am alarm canceled".

- If an alarm is on and you request another alarm for 7am, Alexa will say, "Second alarm set for 7am," and both alarms will show on the App, and on a screen if applicable.

- For repeating alarms, say, "Set an alarm for":

    — — 6am every day

    — — 2pm every Friday

    — — 7:30am on weekends

- If you forget to specify AM or PM, Alexa will ask, "Is that 6 in the morning or the evening?" and you can reply without using the wake word as long as your Alexa-enabled device is still listening.

- If you don't respond, Alexa will ask again after a few seconds, and if you don't respond to the second query, no alarm will be set.

- All Alarms will appear on the main Alarms page on the App with boxes turned On/ Off, indicators shown such as "Every day," with On alarms listed first.

Managing Alarms manually:

- Once you've created an alarm using your voice, go to **Reminders & Alarms** in the App and select **Alarms**.

- Use the box next to any alarm to turn it On and Off as desired.

- Select any Alarm to edit it, and a page will display where you can edit the Time, the Alarm Sound, and choose Repeats options including Never and Delete the alarm if you wish.

- When you've edited the alarm, select **Save Changes** or **Cancel**.

Managing Alarm Volume & Sound manually:

- On your PC or Mac **Manage alarm volume and default sound** from the main Alarms page, and you'll be taken to a page in Settings (though here, we discuss just sounds related to Alarms); on the App on your mobile there is a Settings link at the bottom of the page for the alarms.

- **Change the Alarm, Timer and Notification Volume** by dragging the button on the slide bar on your PC or Mac (note that this does not change the volume for any other device function) or swiping right or left on a tablet or mobile phone.

- Under Custom Sounds, the **Alarm** box will show the Alarm Default Sound, which can be changed by expanding the box using the > shaped caret on your PC or Mac, or by simply tapping on the current Custom Sound.

- **On your PC or Mac**, **Manage alarm volume and default sound** from the main Alarms page, and you'll be taken to a page in Settings (though here, we discuss just sounds related to Alarms); on the App on your mobile there is a Settings link at the bottom of the page for the alarms.

CJ's Tips: If you set up an alarm to go off at the same time every day of the week you won't be able to cancel that alarm for just one day if you don't need it, you have to cancel the whole weekly alarm. Consequently, although it takes me a little longer to set up, I tend to set up an alarm for each day that I need it giving me full control over each alarm.

Also, do check out Celebrity alarm sounds, these change over time and some of them are pretty funny. Failing that, the more traditional alarm sounds are worth exploring to find the one that suits you best; or you can also opt for your favorite song to be the sound that plays for your alarm.

Timers

If you're like me, you'll eventually use Timers for a range of purposes, some which overlap with Reminders. These are simple functions, so this can be quick:

- Timers can be set for 1 second to 24 hours.

- Timers **must** be set with voice, so say, "Set a timer for 45 minutes" or "Cancel the timer".

- You can name a timer so try saying, "Set pizza timer for 10 minutes".

- Multiple timers can be set to run concurrently.

- Active timers will display on an Alexa-enabled device screen for a few seconds at the beginning or if you say, "Show me the timer".

- Active timers will display and count down on the App.

- Note that timers can only be paused through the App; do this by tapping on them when they're displayed on a device with a touch screen, tablet or mobile phone, or by selecting them on your PC or Macc.

- Select **Manage timer volume** to be taken to the Settings page to adjust Alarm, Timer and Notification Volume.

- To turn off a timer, say, "Delete timer" or do it manually on the App.

CJ's Tips: Multiple named timers are so great in the kitchen when you're cooking. Set and name timers for every element of the meal you're making so each timer also becomes a reminder of what's finished cooking or what needs to happen next.

9: Keep it Simple
— Routines

For any voice command you read in this chapter be sure to use your wake word ("Alexa", "Amazon", etc) first.

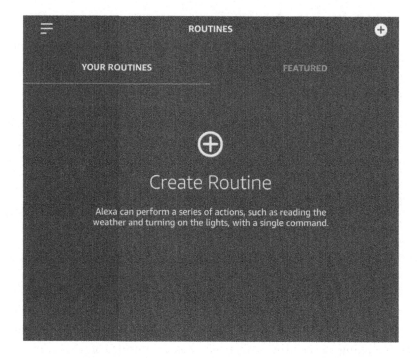

Routines is one of the newer Alexa features, and one I'd been waiting on for quite some time. The number of things that I can do with Alexa and my Echo devices has grown rapidly since their launch. This also means that the amount of time I would spend "talking" to Alexa has grown too. Every time I wanted Alexa to do something I would have to give her a voice command for each thing and sometimes that could be a drag. I previously mentioned in the Lists chapter that if I want to add items to my shopping list by voice then I have to do it one item at a time... "Alexa add oranges to my list," "Alexa, add apples to my list," "Alexa, add bananas to my list" etc, etc. If I have 20 items to add to my shopping list this can get really old, really quickly.

Well, although the **Routines** feature doesn't yet solve that little conundrum it is a step in the right direction and shows me that Amazon is now addressing the question of how to activate several functions at once with just one voice command.

So here's the idea of Routines. We all have daily habits and routines, from getting up and dressed in the morning to coming home from work and cooking dinner in the evening. Now you can group certain Alexa features together to compliment those daily routines and have them all start/activate at the same time, either with one single voice command or at a set time each day.

For example, if you wake up at the same time each day you can program a morning routine for Alexa to turn up your thermostat, turn on your Smart Home kettle, give you the weather forecast and catch you up on news headlines via your Flash Briefing. Either set this routine to start at 6.30 am every morning or start the routine by saying something like "Alexa, start the day" or "Alexa, good morning" or whatever you like!

So that's the good news about Routines. The slightly less good news is that, at the time of writing, the actions that you can program as part of a routine are limited to playing music, Smart Home devices, your calendar, your Flash Briefing, your traffic information and a weather forecast. Personally, while I do use Alexa's news, traffic and weather features, they are not so important to me that I need to schedule them for a set time each day. Bunching the operation of several Smart Home devices into one request is certainly welcome but I already have the ability to do that via Smart Home Groups (discussed later in this guide).

So Routines is a great idea and one that I think will become very useful in the future as more options are added. I'm hoping that it won't be too long before Reminders or are added to the list, as that would be a very useful thing to hear first thing in the day, along with the weather report and the radio playing.

Another thing to note, is that at the time of writing, I could only access the **Routines** page of the App via my tablet and mobile — and not via my PC.

For now, let's look at how to setup a routine. Go into your Alexa App on a mobile device and tap the **Menu icon** (top left) and then **Routines**. You will see that Alexa has some suggested Featured routines. For now, ignore this and tap the big + Create Routine in the middle the page, of the + sign at the top right of the page.

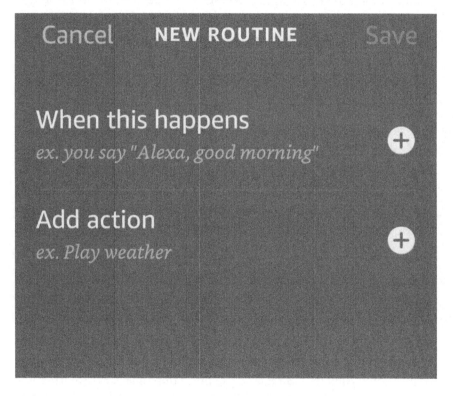

Now you will have the options to **When this happens** and **Add action**. Tap the + **sign** next to **When this happens** and chose and option — the obvious being either to create a voice command for your routine (example, "Alexa, good morning") or schedule a set time for your routine. When scheduling a time, you not only set the time of day but can choose to have the routine happen on a specific day, every day, week days or weekends. You can also link your routine to a certain

Smart Home device activating, or the pressing of an Echo Button, or for when you dismiss a particular alarm.

Follow the prompts to save what cue or condition is used to activate the routine. Don't forget to press Save when you're done.

Now tap the **+ *sign*** next to ***Add action***. You will now be able to choose from the options I mentioned earlier, ***Music, News, Smart Home, Traffic, Weather*** or ***Alexa Says*** (this last option is quite fun – offering a number of stock phrases that Alexa can use to reply to your Routine opener). There is also an option to set the volume for your Routine feature marked ***Audio Control***. Setting up some of these features is discussed in the relevant chapters of this guide. For now, all you need to know is that you can tap ***Add*** to include one or all of these features to your new Routine and then tap ***Create***.

You may also be prompted to choose which Alexa enabled device plays the routine, if you have more than one Echo for example. Again, don't forget the tap on Save when you've got everything set up how you want.

Your new routine will now appear in your list of routines and you can tap again on any routine to edit it, temporarily toggle the routine on or off, and delete the routine if you wish. I suggest you read on now and return to this chapter when you have read the **Smart Home chapter** and the **Things to Try** chapter where I discuss linking Smart Home devices to Alexa and setting up news, traffic and weather briefings.

CJ's Tips: In the upcoming Smart Home chapter I discuss how to put several Smart Home devices into Groups for convenience. One thing that Routines can do, that Smart Home Groups can't, is to activate a number of devices at a set time of the day (or night). This is an aspect of Routines that is already very useful for me. I like certain lights in my home to come on and switch off at certain times of the day, especially when I am away from home to give the impression that the house is still occupied. Scheduling these lighting states for set times and on set days is now a breeze with Alexa Routines.

10: Let's See What She Can Do — Alexa Skills

For any voice command you read in this chapter be sure to use your wake word ("Alexa", "Amazon", etc) first.

Alexa Skills are like "apps" for your Alexa-enabled devices. In the same way that you download apps to your tablet or phone for added functionality, you can add (enable) Skills for Alexa that allow you to do more and get more out of your device. Adding and using these skills is super easy and there are currently more than 70,000 Skills to choose from, and the number grows daily! Skills are loosely grouped into 23 categories currently. Some are good, many are bad, there are sure to be a few of interest for every Alexa user. For an overview of Alexa Skills visit: https://amzn.to/2pN2hC5

Get Familiar with Skills

Start your Skills adventure by getting to know what's available. There are three ways to browse Skills, and all begin on the **Skills** page on the Alexa App Menu (**Skills & Games** on the mobile App version).

This is one area of the Alexa App that I think is easier to deal with on your PC or Mac, since there are so many Skills to consider having a larger screen to view them on makes it easier. So, ideally on your PC or Mac, you'll see that the default setting on the **Skills** landing page is to show All Skills. Near the top right is a tab called Your Skills, which will be populated as you enable Skills for your use. Once you are adding Skills, you'll likely toggle back and forth between the All Skills and Your Skills lists quite a bit. OK, let's explore starting on the **Skills** page in the Alexa App.

If you access the App via your mobile, the **Skills & Games** landing page defaults to a page called Discover skills that has various rotating and scrollable tabs that link to information about certain Skills or skills categories. Along the top of the landing page you'll also see where to go to search for skills via Categories; and a link to Your Skills, which will be populated once you've enabled some.

So, here's how to find Skills that will enhance your Alexa experience

Option 1: *Scan the rows/ tabs of Skills* on the *All Skills* or *Discover Skills* landing page

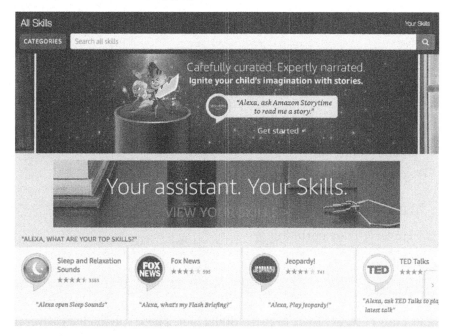

Option 2: Explore the *Categories tab* where Skills are organized in over 20 categories including:

- Newest Arrivals

- Business & Finance

- Communication

- Connected Car

- Education & Reference

- Food & Drink

- Games, Trivia & Accessories
- Health & Fitness
- Home Services
- Kids
- Lifestyle
- Local
- Movies & TV
- Music & Audio
- News
- Novelty & Humor
- Productivity
- Shopping
- Smart Home
- Social
- Sports
- Travel & Transportation
- Utilities
- Weather

Select any category to browse the Skills in it. There will likely be several Skills and you can organize your browsing by choosing the "Sort by" options to the right of the results (Relevance, Customer Rating, Release Date or Featured).

CJ's Tips: For some categories there may be way too many Skills to scroll through can be a long list! Currently, there are over 900 Skills in the Health & Fitness category, so rather than scrolling through the options, I used the search box to narrow the list to skills related to a personal interest such as biking. Sixteen results appeared. If there were still too many results, I would use the "Sort by" options to narrow the search further.

Option 3: Use the Search box to find a Skill for something very specific (e.g., ecobee, weather Canada, Corvette) or to see if there is one related to one of your interests. For a random sampling, I typed in:

- "Chinese" and received 72 search results related to learning the language or one of the dialects, cuisine, the Chinese calendar and zodiac, etc.

- "Flowers" — 40 results about ordering flowers, facts and trivia, state flowers, etc.

- "Michigan" — 46 results about trivia, history, several state universities, winning lottery numbers, snow reports for skiing, information from news outlets, etc.

The results can be narrowed using the "Sort by" options at the top right of the results list or by adding a word or two to your search query — "Chinese language", or "University of Michigan", for example. For something like "news" with over 2500 results, you'll have to search a specific news organization, news about a topic, city, event or similarly narrow term.

Enable Alexa Skills and Use Them

Skills are super easy to set up and use. There's no downloading required and most can be activated just with your voice if you know what you're looking for. When you're ready to put a Skill into action, the first step is to enable it, which is like turning it on for use with your Alexa account and Alexa-enabled devices.

Here's how to enable and use an Alexa Skill:

- Use one of the options above to locate a skill you want to enable, and select the skill. A full-page description for that particular skill will appear.

- Select **Enable Skill**, and after a few seconds, the box will switch to

Disable Skill, which means it's been enabled and will appear in the Your Skills list.

- Note that you might be required to link the Skill to your Amazon account, in which case follow the prompts to do so – this will usually require you to log into your Amazon account

- Alternately, say, "Enable the Rainforest Sounds Skill" (for example).

- You can also browse and Enable Skills on Amazon.com (https:// amzn.to/2ONKNni)

- To use any Enabled Skill, include the name of the Skill and make a request such as "Play rainforest sounds".

- **Note:** Skills in use do not appear on the *Now Playing* page or *Player*, so to control them, say "Stop," "Pause," "Resume" or similar.

Get the Most from the Skills You Enable

The more familiar you are with the Skill's capabilities, the more it will benefit you. Here are suggestions for optimizing a Skill's usefulness:

- If another action is offered along with Enabling the Skill, such as Manage in News Briefing (common for Skills from news organizations, and covered later), select the option to learn about it and decide whether to use the feature.

- Read the *About the Skill* section to acquaint yourself with its capabilities.

- Review the *Try Saying* suggestions to get the Skill to do what you want and additional suggestions in the About information.

- Learn the *Invocation Name* for the Skill (found under Skill Details) to be sure Alexa will put it to work when you want to use it.

- Browse the *Customers Have Also Enabled* section for similar or complementary ideas.

- Read reviews, and, if interested, add a review after you've used the Skill for a few weeks.

- Select *Having Trouble with This Skill* to get help using it from the source of the Skill.

Disable an Alexa Skill

Over time, the Your Skills section can become crowded with Skills you don't use. They're easy to remove.

- Select the skill from Your Skills list

- Select **Disable Skill**, and the box will flip to Enable Skill to indicate it isn't enabled and the Skill will disappear from your list

CJ's Tips: It's important to note that some of the Skills require creating and/ or linking to an account or subscription separate from Amazon, so additional steps might be required. This is just as straightforward as the account linking that you would have done for some of the music services described in Chapter 5. For example, if you want to order an Uber cab or a Domino's pizza then you will need to link Alexa to the accounts you hold with those companies. Clicking the **Enable** button will automatically open a window for you to sign in to your account or set one up if you don't yet have one.

While you're on the full description page for a Skill, and before you enable it, take a moment to familiarize yourself with what it offers, how it works and what others think about it. It's very tempting, when you first start browsing Skills, to go a bit crazy and start enabling dozens of new skills straight away... I don't recommend it... you just end up with lots of Skills that you either don't like, don't know how to use or forget that you even have!

I always read the following...

- **About this Skill:** You might be surprised how often your expectation of what a Skill will do is very different from what it actually does.

- **Try Saying:** Pay attention to these commands as they are probably the only ones that work, so you'll need to remember them.

- **Invocation Name:** Found under "Skill Details", you will certainly need to remember the invocation name of the Skill as this is the name that Alexa is listening for to identify the Skill you're trying to use.

- **Reviews:** It's definitely worth checking out the best and worst reviews of a Skill. I like to see at least a dozen reviews for any given Skill and a star rating of 4 stars and above. I will look at skills with lower star ratings if I think the Skill is going to be really useful. The Domino's Pizza Skill is a good example. It has a lot of negative one star reviews from users who couldn't make the Skill work or had a bad experience. I liked the idea of easy voice ordering so gave it a try for myself and it works fine for me... mainly because I always order the same pizza... every time!

CJ's Tips: Whilst researching this book I've explored more than 800 Skills and Enabled more than 500, but my Skills list currently has 48 Skills; I use some daily and others only occasionally.

The Skills I rely on the most are those that save me time, are easy to use and/or offer genuine value. If they're a hassle, a time-waster or not the easiest or best way to do things, I either disable them immediately or as soon as the novelty wears off. Some have features that are easy to use while some have features that are a hassle.

Alexa Skills are still very new and there are quite a few bugs in some that need to be ironed out. My experience is that the simple Skills work best while the more ambitious Skills fall short. For example, quiz Skills and ambient sound Skills deliver what they promise, whereas recipe Skills often come up short, because the technical requirements of searching through an enormous database of recipes and delivering step by step instructions via Alexa appear to be out of reach for the time being.

You'll also notice that there are sometimes several Skills that do the same thing. Searching Skills for "find my phone" yielded seven results, "restaurant finder" showed ten options and "control lights" produced a list of 48 smart home Skills.

When I'm undecided about which of two or three Skills to choose, I enable both or all and use them alternately. I often use one right after another, and do that every day for a week or so. This is a better way to determine which Skill is right for me than to try one for a week and then try another. I like an immediate, one-after-the-other comparison.

The point I'm delicately trying to make is that there are many Skills that... just aren't very good. It's worth putting in some time to find the gems that you'll use over and over, but be prepared to wade through quite a lot of rubbish!

Alexa Skills Blueprint

This is a very recent development at Amazon, and one that I'm looking forward to exploring further. Basically, the idea of Skills Blueprint is that you can use pre-loaded, customizable templates provided by Amazon to create your own unique Skill.

For example, you could set up a care guide for your pet sitter – with feeding instructions and such, or create a trivia game skill about your family history to play at family gatherings; or you could build your own bedtime story – including sound effects – where you and/or your kids are the heroes!

If this is something that appeals to you, go straight to the Amazon Skill Blueprint site at blueprints.amazon.com; click on the template that interests you and follow the instructions to create your very own Skill which is then be associated with the Alexa-enabled devices that are linked to your Amazon account. Simple!

11: 21st Century Living — Smart Home

For any voice command you read in this chapter be sure to use your wake word ("Alexa", "Amazon", etc) first.

If you're already integrating smart technology into your home, then learning to control it with Alexa's help will be one of the easier parts of the curve. If you're new to smart home devices, then I recommend you visit the Amazon Smart Home page (https://amzn.to/2ycpjXD) to familiarize yourself with the possible options.

Connecting your smart home device with the Alexa App has always been fairly straightforward. It's worth noting that, with the launch of the All-new Echo 4th Generation, it's even easier for some smart home devices to connect as this new Echo has a built-in ZigBee smart home hub. The Echo Plus and the Echo Show also have the ZigBee hub. This is great news if you're new to smart home tech, as you don't necessarily need to buy a separate smart home hub!

This means that there are now essentially two possibly ways to connect your device to Alexa: either via ZigBee or via the device's Skill. But before we go into further detail, Amazon suggests we cover a few common-sense security tips for using smart home devices with Alexa, so let's do that first:

- Follow the device's instructions for safe, recommended uses

- Confirm that requests have been carried out — especially tasks related to your home's safety and security (security system, exterior lighting, door locks, garage door, HVAC, appliances, and similar)

- Turn off the microphones on all Alexa-enabled devices if you do not want Alexa to respond to voice commands when safety and security cannot be ensured (such as when adults are away from home)

- Remember that once a device is connected, anyone can use Alexa to control it, so make sure those in your household and guests understand safe operation of smart home devices

CJ's Tips: With regard to setting up smart home devices and Alexa, I find it much easier at the start to do the setup via the Alexa App on my PC – the App interface is just a lot clearer to follow. After setting things up, I am then able to use the App on my tablet to help manage my smart home devices. Note that on the App via a tablet/ mobile phone you need to tap on the icon depicting a house with two switches inside which takes you to a landing page for all your smart home Devices. You cannot get to this page via the Menu on the tablet/ mobile version of the Alexa App.

For the rest of this chapter please note that the instructions given are for when you view the Alexa App via your PC or Mac.

Set Up Smart Home Devices via the ZigBee Hub (Echo Show, All-new Echo 4th Gen & Echo Plus)

ZigBee, if you're wondering, is an industry-standard protocol for connecting smart home devices wirelessly. The majority of smart home products have this protocol, so you're likely to find that your smart home is already compatible for use with the ZigBee hub. You can get a full list of ZigBee certified products here: www.zigbee.org/zigbee-products-2/

Once you've confirmed that your device is compatible with ZigBee, here's what you need to do to connect it to your Echo Show, All-new Echo 4th Gen or Echo Plus:

- Ensure your device is within 30 feet of you Echo.

- Switch on the device, then say "Discover my devices".

- Alexa will confirm which devices have been discovered.

- You can then go into the Alexa App and select **Smart Home > Devices** where you'll see the list of devices that are now linked to

Alexa, and from there you can manage the device's status/ Groups and Scenes (explained further later).

Set Up Smart Home Devices via Skills

If your smart home device is not compatible with ZigBee it can still link to Alexa via the device's Skill. You'll be well-prepared for the information here if you've read the previous chapter and enabled a few Skills.

- **Prepare your smart home device for linking to Alexa:** Verify that your smart home device is compatible with Amazon Alexa, which can be done by searching for it on the Skills page of the Alexa App or Amazon.com, checking the packaging, contacting the manufacturer or viewing its website and looking for the device on the Alexa smart home shopping page that includes all compatible devices (https://amzn.to/2wITbeJ)

- Download the manufacturer's app for the smart home device to any device you're using to manage the Alexa App. Download and install the latest software updates for the smart home device.

- Use the manufacturer's app to set up the smart home device/ equipment on the same Wi-Fi network your Alexa device is on.

- **Select the Skill that goes with your device:** by going to the main **Skills** page on the Alexa app, clicking **Categories**, then **Smart Home** and using the search box to find the relevant Skill. Alternately, Skills can be searched on Amazon.com (https://amzn.to/2ONKNni).

- Read the About information and the Skill Details on the device page that opens to familiarize yourself with its capabilities such as viewing a smart home camera on Echo Show.

- Select the **Enable** button, and when it changes to **Disable**, you'll know the Skill is enabled.

- When prompted, sign into the smart home device account to link it to your Alexa account. Follow any further prompts given to complete setting up the smart home device on Alexa.

- **Ask Alexa to Discover the Device:** Say, "Discover devices" or go to the **Smart Home** page on the App, select **Devices**, and then select the **Discover** tab.

Set Up Groups and Scenes for Your Smart Home Devices

Once you've connected smart home devices to Alexa (either via the Skill or via ZigBee), you can then set them up to work together by putting them into groups or scenes.

It may seem at first that there is no real difference between the Group option and the Scenes option; but in fact they have different functions.

Basically, when your smart home devices are put together in a Group the command you can give them via Alexa is simply to turn those devices on or off simultaneously, so for example turning on three specific light bulbs in the bedroom at the same time.

However, the Scenes option allows you to predetermine the state of those devices, for example if you want the light bulbs to be on low and the thermostat to go down to a lower temperature at bedtime (in this case the Scene would be named Bedtime and the command to Alexa would be "Alexa, turn on Bedtime").

The other big difference is that you set up a Group within the Alexa App; whereas to set up Scenes you need to first configure those scenes in the smart home device's app, and then those specific device scenes will be listed in the Scenes page on the Alexa App, where you can then control those scenes via Alexa.

Effectively the *Scenes* page simply shows you the different scenes you have already set up and then allows you to manage them with Alexa voice commands.

How to Set Up Groups:

Chose the *Groups* tab on the main *Smart Home* page.

- Choose *Create Group* to connect two or more devices that will work together with a single command.

- Follow any additional prompts to complete formation of the Group including naming the group and selecting devices for the group.

- Try the Group by making a request of Alexa appropriate to the Group's functionality ("Turn on the lights," or "Lock the doors," for example).

- To edit the Group, select it and choose the name to change it or select/deselect devices you want in the group.

- To delete a group, select *Delete this group*.

CJ's Tips: Alexa uses voice recognition to understand what you say and connect it with digital content such as the name of a group you type into the App. For this reason, give groups names that won't confuse Alexa. To be on the safe side, I recommend sticking with the Common Group names that Alexa offers.

How to Manage Scenes:

First configure specific Scenes within the smart home device's app. For example, if you want to create a scene with the Philips Hue smart light, then you need to go into the Hue app to set up that scene.

Then choose the *Scenes* tab on the main *Smart Home* page:

- All Scenes that you have set up on your smart home devices should appear, meaning that you can use voice command to activate those Scenes, using the name you've set for that Scene ("turn on Bedtime" for example).

- If you don't want Alexa to control a certain Scene, then click on **Forget** to delete the Scenes from the Alexa App.

Troubleshooting Alexa and Smart Home Device Set Up

If Alexa doesn't discover your smart home device, try these tips in this order. They will troubleshoot and solve most issues.

Device Issues: Double-check that:

- Your smart home device is compatible with Alexa.

- That you have Enabled the device's Skill.

- That you have downloaded the device's app.

- That you have downloaded the latest software updates for the device.

- For a Philips Hue Bridge, be sure to press the button on the Bridge before trying to discover devices.

Note: Additional details for these steps are found in the four steps above.

- Restart your Alexa-enabled device, and restart your smart home device.

- Disable and Enable the smart home device.

- In the Alexa App, choose the Forget option for the smart home device to unlink it from Alexa, and then try to reconnect it.

Wi-Fi Issues: Your Alexa-enabled device and your smart home devices must be on the same Wi-Fi network. Personal networks are best; school and work networks you don't control might not allow unrecognized devices to connect.

Check or change the Wi-Fi network for your Alexa-enabled device by:

- Choosing the Settings page for your device.

- Observing what network your device is on beneath the Wi-Fi option.

- Changing the Wi-Fi network, if necessary.

- Using the Add a Network option to add a network for device and smart home devices.

Note: Some smart home devices can only connect to the 2.4 GHz Wi-Fi band. If you have a dual-band network, make sure it is set to the 2.4 GHz band.

Change confusing group names: Alexa won't comprehend words with numbers or symbols in them like kitch3n lights or #kitchen lights@, so make changes to group names, if necessary.

Discover your smart home devices again: If you've made any changes discussed here, including the Wi-Fi network or band or a group name say, "Discover devices." Alexa will let you know if they are found or will say "I didn't find any devices." If this occurs, contact the smart home device manufacturer for further assistance, since it is up to the device manufacturer, not Amazon, to ensure that their devices are compatible with Alexa devices.

How to Disconnect Smart Home Devices from Alexa

A list of your smart home Devices will populate the Smart Home main page. Select any of the Devices and then select *Forget it* to disconnect it from Alexa.

Note about Migrating from an Existing Hub to the ZigBee Hub

If you have been using smart home devices for some time, you may already have a main smart home hub where you can control things like Groups and Routines. You may be more than happy with this setup, but if you find that your devices are also ZigBee compatible, you might want to switch to the ZigBee hub in your Echo and streamline the hardware in your home.

To do this you have to first remove the devices from the existing hub and from Alexa (which might have been linked to via the device's Skill), and then reconnect. Here are the steps to follow:

- Go to the app associated with your existing smart home hub and remove or forget the device from the hub.

- Then, go into the Alexa App and select **Smart Home > Devices,** choose the device in question and then select **Forget** this device

- Then, go into **Skills > Your Skills** and disable the Skill that was linked to the device.

- Finally, switch off the old hub so that there's no interference and then reconnect to the ZigBee hub as per the instructions above. If you have any trouble with this, you might have to reset the smart home device to its original factory settings.

Of course, if you still have other devices connected to your old hub, then you can switch that back on once you're sure the devices you want to connect via ZigBee are fully migrated.

Alexa Hunches

This is a relatively recent feature to help manage your smart home devices; it is optional, but is on by default.

The basic premise of the Hunch feature is that Alexa will let you know if any of your smart home devices isn't in the state you need it to be to complete a request. For example, if you have a nighttime Scene request such as "Goodnight" which should mean that all your smart lights are turned off, but one light isn't responding, then Alexa will let you know and possibly offer a solution.

Alexa provides hunches for connected smart home devices such as, plugs, lights, locks, and switches. If you find the Hunch feature annoying, you can turn it off by saying "disable Hunches" or in the App go to **Settings > Hunches** and toggle off there.

12: Your Highly Capable Personal Assistant — Things to try

For any voice command you read in this chapter be sure to use your wake word ("Alexa", "Amazon", etc) first.

This is a large section of the Alexa App and could almost be a book of its own!

The good news is that many of the **Things to Try** have been discussed in other sections, and the ones I don't talk about anywhere are very straightforward and easy to use with the few words of explanation given in the Alexa App. Our purpose in this chapter is to shed light on Things to Try that haven't been mentioned but require some explanation.

To get started, select **Things to Try** from the menu in the Alexa App to explore them for yourself or to follow along with this discussion. The interface of the Alexa App for this page is quite different when viewed on a tablet or mobile phone compared to a PC or Mac. On a PC or Mac, the Things to Try section is just a list of items, whilst on a tablet or mobile phone the list is presented with both words and icons for each item.

I have also noticed that there appear to be many more Things to Try items listed on the tablets and mobile phones version, than on the PC or Mac version of this page – an indication, perhaps, that more and more users are primarily accessing the Alexa App on their mobile devices.

Either way, when you select any of the items on the list, you will usually be taken to the **Help & Feedback** section for an explanation. The list serves as an easy place to find topics you want more information about.

Here are some of the useful and interesting **Things to Try** that haven't been detailed already in the book:

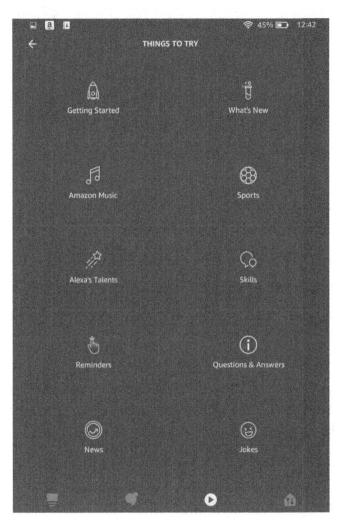

What's new?

I like to keep up with Alexa's capabilities, so I check this section weekly, at least. There's always something new. It's a mixed and disorganized bag ranging from simple, fun stuff ("Drum roll") to interesting information (the ability to give publication dates and authors for popular books) to new Skills ("Give me a quote") to new Alexa-enabled devices. It's a potpourri of fresh possibilities with Alexa.

Ask Questions

If you can think it, the question might be worth asking. I ask these types of questions quite often:

- What time it is here or elsewhere?
- Conversions of weight, measurements temperature, money.
- Spellings/ synonyms/ definitions.
- People and place fact.
- Math.

Check and Manage Your Calendar

Alexa can link to calendars from Google, Apple and Microsoft.

- Go to Settings, and scroll down the Account section to Calendars.
- Choose the calendar you want to connect, and select Link _____ account.
- Link another calendar, if desired.
- If your device has a screen, say, "Show me my calendar." If not just ask, "What's on my calendar," "What's my next appointment" or similar.
- Say, "Add a 9:30am meeting to my calendar".

Discover New Alexa Skills

See the Chapter 10 dedicated to Alexa Skills, but if you want to hear about the latest releases:

- Say, "What are popular Skills?".
- Say, "What new Skills do you have?".
- Browse the Skills store mentioned earlier where every Skill can be found and Enabled (https://amzn.to/2ONKNni).

Printing with Alexa

If you're in the market for a new printer, then be sure to get one that is compatible with Alexa (most IPP-enabled network connected printers manufactured by HP, Brother, Canon, and Epson - there should be the mention "Works with Alexa" on the printer product page).

Then you can ask Alexa to print out a number of items using various Alexa features and skills (for example your Shopping List, coloring pages, sudoku puzzles, recipes (in conjunction with the allrecipes Sklll), educational worksheets and more...

Find out more about compatible skills and exactly what Alexa can print for you here: https://amzn.to/32Ryege

Once you have a compatible printer, get started by asking Alexa to "discover my printer" or go to **Devices > Add Device > Printer**. Note that if you want to deselect your printer, you'll need to do it via the App and not by voice.

Once linked to a printer Alexa will also notify you when the ink or toner is low, and let you know if it's time to reorder more. To turn off that particular notification then go to **Devices > Select Printer > Status > Change >Turn off notifications**.

Alternatively, you can also set up a smart reorder so that new printer ink and toner is automatically ordered when Alexa notices that they are low. To do this go to **Devices > Select Printer > Status > Change > Automatically reorder when supply is low**.

Find Local Business and Restaurants

If you haven't set your location yet, this is a good time to do that, so Alexa knows where to search. On your PC or Mac go to **Settings**, select your device. In the **General** section of the Alexa App, select **Device location** and **Edit**, if the location is incorrect. Add as little as your zip code or as much as your full address. The more information you provide, the more accurate Alexa can be in telling you how far you are from businesses and restaurants.

Note that this task can be done on the App via a mobile/ tablet by going to **Menu > Settings > Device settings**. Then choose your device and scroll down to **Device location**. Select that option and you can enter or change your address there. Don't forget to tap Save when you're done.

Now you can ask Alexa to help you find local businesses. With some Alexa-enabled devices that have screens, results will be displayed on the screen, with the business name, a short description, its distance from your location and Yelp rating with number of reviews. To see more results, slide the screen left. Use the touch screen to select a listing for its street address, phone number and business hours, if available.

Here are things to try:

- "Find a Mexican restaurant."
- "Is the post office open?"
- "What clothing stores are nearby?"
- "What supermarkets are near me?"
- "What is the phone number for B&V Asian Market?"

Your search doesn't have to be local either. When planning a trip, you can ask Alex to find any of these things in another town.

- "Is there a shoe store in Grand Rapids?"
- "Pharmacy in Plano, Texas"
- "Is there Crossfit in Raleigh, North Carolina?"

As well as Alexa reporting the result of your search to you, all searches produce Cards, so you'll have the results right in front of you on the Alexa App with detailed information including, where applicable Yelp ratings.

Search results might be varied, especially when there are few good options. When using Alexa in a rural area, I requested a "sporting goods store," and got one accurate result and four others ranging from a used firearms dealer to a marina. See you how do with your searches!

CJ's Tips: Alexa is far from perfect yet, but I'm often impressed with the information I can get from her. If I need to call a local shop or business I always ask Alexa for the number first before reaching for the phone book or doing a search online; more often than not, I get the info I'm looking for.

Find Traffic Information

Alexa can give you an estimated time for your commute and the fastest route.

- In **Settings** on the Alexa App, scroll down and select **Traffic**.

- Add or change your current address, your "From"

- Add a destination, your "To"

- Stops along the way can be added too.

- Later, select **Change address** to edit any of the locations.

Once set, you can then ask Alexa, "What's my traffic?". While I use this for the drive I make most often, it can be convenient for determining the time for other driving routes by changing the "From," "To" or both.

Get Weather Forecasts

Once Alexa knows your location in **Settings > Your Device > Device location**, you can hear or view local weather information on your devices screen, if appropriate, and on the Card produced within the App. Ask about weather in other cities around the globe too. Common questions Alexa can answer include:

- "What's the weather?"

- "Will it rain tomorrow?"

- "How warm will it be today?"

There are many ways to answer the question, but Alexa replies to all of them with the same information — verbally sharing current and expected weather conditions for the next 24 hours and showing an extended forecast.

Go to the Movies

This section uses your location to access local movie schedules and can give you information for movie schedules in cities you'll be visiting. I get the best results with questions like these:

- "What movies are playing?"

- "What movies are playing at [name of theater complex]?"

- "When will Indiana Jones play tomorrow?"

- "Tell me about the Aquaman movie"

Note that with Alexa-enabled devices that have screens, you can also Alexa to show you trailers of the movie that you are interested in.

Hear the News

Alexa offers something called a **Flash Briefing**. Many news and entertainment organizations including NPR, NBC, FOX, BBC and ESPN make brief overviews of the news, such as you might hear at the top or bottom of the hour, and those summaries can be added to your Flash Briefing.

To select which summaries you want to hear in your Briefing, and to start and manage it:

- Go to **Settings** > **Alexa Preferences** > **Flash Briefing** to toggle On or Off the default options, if there are any.

- If not, go to **Skills** and search your favorite news, sports, weather and entertainment stations (there are new media coming on board every week), and enable the Skill.

- If it offers a Briefing summary, that will show in your list of Flash Briefing choices in Settings.

- Toggle On or Off the briefings, and you can make changes when desired.

- Ask "What's the news," "Give me my flash briefing," "Flash briefing," "What's in the news?" or something similar, and you'll hear the entire briefing, one organization at a time.

- If the news organization offers video with its briefing, it will play on Alexa-enabled devices that have screens.

Note: The briefing does not show on the Now Playing page or the Player.

CJ's Tips: Once you've toggled the briefings ON, a blue Edit Order options will appear at the top of the page. Click on this and then tap/click and drag each of your news sources into your preferred order of importance. I find that there are a couple of news sources I value above the others, so I definitely want to hear them first. Don't forget to tap/click Done when you're finished to preserve the order you've chosen.

Get Your Sports Updates

Give Alexa a team name and say, "score," and you'll hear the score of the most recent game. If you want to hear the latest scores and the next game for all the teams you follow, go to **Settings > Sports Update** to search and select those teams. Then, you'll get the answer when you ask questions like:

- "What's my Sports Update."

- "When do the Seattle Mariners play next?"

- "NBA scores."

- "Score for Real Madrid."

- "How many touchdowns did Odell Beckham junior score?"

- "How many homeruns does Aaron Judge have?"

Many major football, baseball, basketball and soccer leagues are currently supported on the Alexa App, including:

North American Leagues:

- MLB — Major League Baseball

- MLS — Major League Soccer

- NBA — National Basketball Association

- NCAA — National Collegiate Athletic Association

- NFL — National Football League

- NHL — National Hockey League

- WNBA — Women's National Basketball Association

European Leagues:

- English Premier League

- FA Cup — Football Association Challenge Cup

- German Bundesliga

- UEFA Champions League

CJ's Tips: Above is a list of all the teams officially supported via Alexa, but I've found that I can get information for many other teams just by searching for them in the search box at **Settings > Sports Update** within the Alexa App.

Set Up a TV Schedule

Never miss an episode again! This is neat little feature if you like to keep track of when your favorite TV is on.

Go to **Settings> Alexa Preferences >TV Schedules**. Then tap on the words TV Provider and scroll the options until you find your provider of choice (if it's not there, then that provider is not available yet on this feature).

Select your provider and tap OK. Now this is set up, you can ask Alexa about the TV schedule on that provider, and then use Alexa to set a

Reminder (see Chapter 8) so that you don't forget to watch or record your show

Shop Amazon (for Prime Members)

Did you hear about the 6-year old girl in Texas who ordered a dollhouse with Alexa or Jimmy Kimmel's prank of telling Alexa to order pool noodles during his show broadcast into millions of US homes?

These are cautionary tales about shopping via Alexa, but with precautions, you'll be immune from such surprises.

To shop on Amazon, you'll need:

- A Prime membership (a 30-day free trial is available).

- A US shipping address.

- A payment method stored with Amazon in your account's 1-Click settings.

- Voice Purchasing enabled in the Alexa App at **Settings > Alexa Account > Voice Purchasing**.

- (Optional) A 4-digit code in **Settings > Alexa Account > Voice Purchasing** that you'll have to give as a safeguard against unauthorized shopping, accidental purchases and not-so-funny pranks.

- Use Manage 1-Click Settings in this section to be sure you have a payment method connected to 1-Click.

- An Alexa-enabled device and the Alexa App.

Once you're set up, you can order Prime-eligible items with Alexa. If your Alexa-enabled device also has a screen you can browse shopping items visually too, or you can also browse via the Alexa App **Homepage** and order Prime-eligible items with Alexa. Here's how my shopping with Alexa usually goes when I'm not sure which product I want:

- I say, "Shop coffee makers," and then browse them on the screen or in the App.

- I select Details of any product to learn more including color options, sizes.

- When I make the decision to buy, I select "Buy This," and the order is placed.

- If I get buyer's regret immediately, I say, "Cancel my order", and it's cancelled.

- Canceling orders after a longer time must be done online.

- When the order ships, Alexa gives me a voice notification that also shows up in *Settings > Notifications*.

When I know what I want, the process is much shorter:

- "Order _____," and Alexa will ask you to confirm the order or will show several options on your Alexa-enabled device screen.

- "Reorder _____," and Alexa will ask for confirmation.

- "Add _____ to my cart," is an option too, and you can then go online to review your cart and place the order.

You can also buy digital music with Alexa if you have a US billing address and payment method stored with Amazon that is issued by a US bank. Amazon.com gift cards can be used too.

Physical goods ordered can be tracked with a simple request, "Track my order."

Calling and Messaging

This feature has tremendous potential and will become more useful as the universe of Alexa users expands. If you know three or more people with Alexa-enabled devices, this section might be worth reading now. Otherwise, it's here when Alexa catches on more broadly among your friends, family members and business contacts. You can communicate with other Alexa users if you both have downloaded the Alexa App (note that you don't necessarily need to have a specific Amazon Echo device to download the Alexa App onto your phone), and inputted the contact's information correctly.

Note that at the time of writing, I could only access this section of the Things to Try through my tablet and mobile phone, so I suggest that this is how you do it too.

Setting up Calling and Messaging

- Ensure you have the Alexa App on your tablet of mobile phone.

- Download the latest Alexa App for iOS 9.0 or higher here: https://apple.co/2xhWycQ

- Or for Android 5.0 or higher here: https://bit.ly/2fBWcUi

- Select the Conversations icon (a speech bubble) at the bottom of the page, and follow the instructions to sign up for Alexa Calling & Messaging and to verify your mobile number.

- Import your contacts, and those who have signed up for Calling and Messaging will appear in your **Contacts** list.

- To add or edit contacts for this service, update your phone's local Address book and then open the Alexa App.

- Give your contacts names you'll remember, ask Alexa to call one of them, and Alexa will dial the number associated with that name.

- Calling and Messaging can be used on Echo, Echo Show, Echo Dot, Echo Auto and Fire Tablet with Alexa, or between non-Echo users that have the Alexa App on their phone.

- Note that some Echo devices with a screen offer a video calling option.

- If you ever wish to deregister from Calling and Messaging, contact Amazon customer service at 1.877.375.9365.

Using Calling and Messaging for Calls

- Tell your Alexa-using friends and family about Calling and Messaging, and encourage them to get set up.

- To make a call from your device say, "Call Aunt Ellen," and Alexa will begin the call.

- If you have the option for video calling select the Video icon on your device's touch screen; if the device goes to default video calling, and you prefer not to use video, say, "Turn video off."

- To make a call from the Alexa App, select the Conversations icon, select a contact and the Phone icon for an audio-only call or the Camera icon for a video call, if applicable.

- When someone is calling you, Alexa will let you know who is calling.

- To answer a call, say, "Answer" or select the Answer button on the devices screen, if applicable.

- To ignore the call, say, "Ignore the call."

- To end a call, say, "Hang up" or tap your touchscreen and select the end-call button.

There's a video about calling with Alexa here: https://amzn. to/2AOKbbf

Using Calling and Messaging for Messages

- Messages are recorded and played back to the recipient rather than transcribed and read by Alexa.

- To send a message, say, "Send a message to Sara Smith," and Alexa will prompt you for the message and send your message when you complete it.

- To send a message from the Alexa App, select the Conversations icon, choose a contact and then select the Keyboard icon; type a message before hitting the Send button.

- To reply to a message from the App, select the conversation from those shown, and press the Microphone icon while speaking your message, releasing it when done to send the message or sliding left to cancel the message.

- To hear messages, say, "Play my messages."

- When more than one phone number is synced with Alexa, you can name the numbers and say, "Play messages for _____" to hear only your messages.

- To review messages on the App, go to Conversations to view those with a New Notification icon, and then choose between hearing the messages and reading a transcription of them.

There's a video about messaging with Alexa here: https://amzn. to/2vqMD2n

Drop in

- Drop in is typically set up among devices in a single household, between family members and BFFs.

- Drop in means that people in separate parts of the home or in different homes can communicate immediately without making a formal call, (and it allows you to see what's going on in the kids' room when two or more Alexa-enabled screen devices are connected).

- To drop in on one of your own devices in your home, say something like, "Drop in on my living room Echo" – when you ask this for the first time, Alexa will ask you if you want to turn on or enable the Drop In feature.

- Friends and family with Alexa can also drop in on each other, but you must both first enable Drop In in your **Contacts** list. Go to the **Contacts** section of the App, select a contact and turn On the Drop-in button if you want them to have drop-in privileges with you. Note that, on the Communications page of the Alexa App on a mobile device you can also see your **Contacts** by tapping the icon of a person on the top right corner of the page.

- Permission can be granted with some screen devices by saying "Show my contacts" and using the touch screen to select the contact and toggle on the drop in option, which can be turned off just as easily.

There's more information about Drop In here: https://amzn. to/3lIXpsY

Announcements

A relatively new addition to the options for Calling and Messaging, the Announcements option works like a one-way intercom where you can basically announce a short message, such as "Dinner's ready!" or "I'm one my way home" to other Alexa enabled devices on your account. For example, from your Echo Show that's in your kitchen to the Echo Dot that's in your kid's room and the Echo that's in the home office. Or from your Alexa App on your mobile phone back to your Echo devices at home.

This is basically similar to Drop In, but just for short voice-only messages. Or you could think of it as a voice version of a text message! Here's how to do it:

- You can use your voice to make an announcement, say "Announce (Dinner's ready!)" and your other enabled Alexa devices will chime and play the announcement.

- Alternatively, manually on the App you can select the Communication icon, then the Announce icon (a loudspeaker) and then type in your message or opt for the microphone to record it; finish by selecting the arrow icon to send.

- Note that mobile devices with the Alexa App (ie your mobile phone) and Echo Auto can send but not receive announcements.

While I've covered the essential details, there is a section on Alexa Calling and Messaging FAQs located here: https://amzn.to/2IEeC8h

Care Hub

During Amazon's launch of the latest Alexa device updates was a new feature called **Care Hub**.

What this essentially does is allow two households that both have Alexa enabled devices be more intimately connected (than say just being Call contacts).

The feature is specifically aimed at those who may have elderly relatives or loved ones that require special care, and will enable them to essentially "check in" with their loved ones, whilst at the same time maintaining a certain level of privacy.

The main options in the Care Hub feature are to give you the ability:

- To see if your loved one has used the Alexa App that day, which effectively suggests that all is well.

- To set up alerts if Alexa is not used in a specific time period.

- To set up an emergency contact link so that if your loved one calls for help, you'll be contacted directly.

- To set up short-cuts for Call or Drop-In.

Amazon stress that this feature does not breach any privacy issues – so for example you can see if your loved one has made a request to Alexa, but not what the request was, and Care Hub can only be activated with consent from both households.

Since many of the voice activated requests that Alexa can do (for example setting up reminders to take pills, getting Alexa to turn on the lights, asking Alexa to play the 'Golden Oldies') are such a boon to anyone with mobility or infirmity issues, this added Care Hub feature could be very welcome.

You can access the Care Hub set up by going to M*enu* > *More* > *Care Hub*. Then follow the prompts to link up your device with your loved one's device. You will need to set up Care Hub on both devices so that they can be linked, and communicate to each other. Once linked up you can choose which features of Care Hub you need most.

Amazon Kids (Formerly FreeTime)

On the *Things to Try* page you'll also see a link to Enable Amazon Kids. This is essentially the parental control section of the App where you can set up Alexa to interact with your kids and ensure that the content they access is appropriate.

Note that you need to enable Amazon Kids only on the Alexa-enabled devices that you want your kids to interact with. So, you'll need to enable it on the device itself – and do so for any and every Alexa-enabled device that you wish to have parental controls on.

So, for example, if your Echo Show is to be used primarily by your kids and you wish to enable Amazon Kids this is what you need to do:

Go to Devices and choose the device (in this case, your Echo Show).

Scroll down and under **General** select **Amazon Kids**. On the next page you'll see a toggle switch set at Disabled – when you toggle it to Enable it you'll be taken to the Amazon Kids landing page where you can then follow the prompts to set up the Amazon Kids service you want and to add child profiles and other basic parental control settings, including setting time limits and filtering out explicit songs.

Note that access to parental controls is part of the free Amazon Kids service; as well as access to a limited range of kid-friendly content for Alexa (such as skills, games and so on).

You will also be given the option to upgrade to the paid-for Amazon Kids+ subscription. At the time of writing Amazon Kids+ cost $2.99 a month for Amazon Prime customers, and $4.99 a month if you don't have Amazon Prime.

There are further advantageous packages depending on whether you prefer the Family Plan which allows up to 4 kids profiles, or want a 3-month or 1-year family plan.

The advantage of Amazon Kids+ for your Echo device is access to many more kid-friendly skills and also ad-free radio stations, and hundreds of Audible books.

The advantage of Amazon Kids+ for other Amazon devices such as the Fire tablet and the Fire TV, is that you can also access lots of kid's TV programs, games and apps, and personalize your kids' profile to give them content customized to their age, interests, learning goals and so on.

You can find out more about managing your Amazon Kids+ subscription here: https://www.amazon.com/ftu/home

Whisper Mode

This is a great feature if you're using an Alexa-enabled device in your kids room (for lullabies for example): you can ask Alexa to recognize your whispered requests, and to whisper back!

The easiest way to do this is to simply enable whisper mode by saying "turn on whisper mode". Alternatively, you can go to **Settings > Alexa Preferences > Voice Responses** and use the toggle switch to enable whisper mode there.

Alexa Guard and Guard Plus

I love this new Alexa feature because it is both kind of amusing and super useful!

The basic Alexa Guard feature acts like a security guard in your home whilst you are out: Alexa listens for preprogramed unusual noises, such as breaking glass, smoke and carbon monoxide detectors, and immediately notifies you via the App on your mobile phone.

Note that the basic Guard will call you in case of trouble – not the emergency services – so it'll then be up to you to react and get the help you need.

A further feature of the basic Guard, is that you can also set it up to communicate with smart home lighting. Alexa Guard will make the lights go on and off in a realistic way when you're not home – genius!

To set up Alexa guard go to **Settings > Alexa Preferences > Guard > Set Up Guard** and then follow the prompts to choose the options you want Alex to listen out for and do.

Then, whenever you leave the house simply say, "I'm leaving," and Alexa will enable Guard; when you return home, say, "I'm home," and Guard will be disabled.

For further home security features, Amazon is soon to release Alexa Guard Plus which is also designed to have greater compatibility with other smart home security systems including Ring, Blink, Arlo or August outdoor cameras, ADT Pulse of Control, and the Scout Alarm system.

Guard Plus will be a paid for subscription ($4.99 per month) and as well as the same features of the basic Guard, the added features will include the ability to place a call (hands-free) to a dedicated Emergency Helpline for assistance; Alexa listening for suspicious activity and sounding a siren when such activity is detected inside; and Alexa making dog baking sounds if motion is detected outside (via smart home cameras/sensors).

I just love the idea of Alexa barking... takes me back to scenes from those Home Alone movies!

Things to Do with Alexa-Enabled Devices with Screens

The following *Things to do* are only relevant if you have an Alexa-enabled device with a screen, such as the Echo Show, the Show 5 & 8 or a Fire Tablet.

Access Silk and Firefox Browsers on the Echo Show

A welcome feature of the new Echo Show 2nd generation is that you can now ask Alexa to go online! Simple say "Open Silk" or "Open Firefox" and the screen will bring up paired down mobile versions of these browsers and a keyboard to type in your search, and a bookmark facility. You are supposed to also be able to ask Alexa for a particular website, for example "Open Wikipedia", but so far, I've found that's been a bit hit and miss. Using the keyboard option is far more efficient and, though I don't really see myself needing to go online on the Echo Show that much, it's good to know it's there. Plus, the browser option provides a useful work around for accessing YouTube since that has been problematic in the past.

Get Recipes and See Step-by-Step Instructions

Amazon has partnered with a number of food/ recipe websites

including Kitchen Stories, Allrecipes, Epicurious, Food52, TheKitchn and SideChef, providing Alexa with a huge catalog of recipes to refer to. Simple ask for a particular recipe, for example "Show me a cookie recipe", and Alexa will find you one and proved step-by-step photos or video on the Echo Show screen! Super news for novice cooks! Note that you may have to enable the Skill for your recipe website of choice (see the Skills chapter to find out how to enable Skills).

See your Amazon Prime Photos (for Prime members)

Amazon Prime includes Amazon Prime Photos, a service that offers unlimited photo storage for you and five other people, whether family or friends, to form a Family Photo Vault. If you're a Prime member, you can learn more by selecting Your Prime Photos from your Account Lists. If you're not an Amazon Prime Member, a 30-day free trial for the can be started from nearly any page of Amazon.com.

FYI, Amazon Prime Photos are stored in the Amazon cloud called Amazon Drive. As mentioned, Prime members get unlimited storage for photos here, and up to 5GB for video storage. There are other subscription plans if you need more storage, to find out more visit the Amazon Drive page. (https://amzn.to/2QGnnxk)

Once you've added photos to your Amazon Prime Photos account, view them on Echo Show devices using the types of commands you'd expect: "Show my photos" or "See my photo vault." Alexa will dialogue with you, and some navigation can be done using the touch screen toop

See your Photo Slideshow

If you wish to view your Amazon Prime Photos as a slideshow on the Echo go to **Settings > Display > Photo Slideshow** and the choose the slideshow speed, then simple say "Show my slideshow" to activate it.

Take Selfies via the Echo Show Photo Booth

With its built-in camera you can take your best selfies via the Echo Show Photo Booth. This fun feature allows you to take Single-shot photos, 4-shot sequences and Sticker-mode shots that include fun overlays in the picture.

- Say, "Take a photo," Alexa will ask you to pick a camera from the single-shot, sticker and 4-shot options that appear. You'll have to touch the screen and slide to the left to get to the 4-shot camera.

- Specify a camera by saying, "Take a single shot," "Take a sticker shot" or "Take a 4-shot photo"

- While Alexa is still in camera mode, make further requests, if desired

If you select Sticker Mode, you'll also need to slide left on the screen to see all options. With practice, you'll be able to frame yourself or your subject with the augmented reality "props." Once you settle on a camera and/or sticker option, Echo Show will count down to the snap of the photo, there will be a brief flash, and if Echo Show isn't muted, a camera sound. Four-shot photos are taken about one second apart, each with its own flash. Photos taken with Echo Show automatically upload to your Amazon Drive account or to Amazon Prime Photos, which can be accessed on the Amazon Drive main page.

To view your Photo Booth images, ask Alexa to "Show my photo albums" and then pick the Photo booth album.

Deleting Images on Echo Show

Annoyingly, you cannot use Echo Show or Alexa to delete any images. To delete either Photo Booth ones or those stored in the Amazon Prime Photos you will have to go into the account directly via Amazon.com or you can also access them via the Prime Photos app (www.amazon.com/photos/apps) that you can download to your mobile device.

Set Photos as a Background on Echo Show

Following on from using Prime Photos with Echo Show, you can change your Echo Show background either to a single photo or using a specific album to create rotating slideshow as the background. To do this by voice, when you are viewing the photo or album you like, simply ask Alexa to "Set this photo/ this album as my background".

To do this manually, go into the Alexa App and select **_Settings > Home Screen Background > Choose a photo/ or Amazon Photos_** and then follow the prompt to choose and save.

13: Tailor-Made Alexa — Settings

For any voice command you read in this chapter be sure to use your wake word ("Alexa", "Amazon", etc) first.

The Settings section is where you control how the Alexa App and your device function to suit your style.

Personally, I prefer to deal with settings functions via the Alexa App on your PC or Mac, where I feel the interface is clearer. The rest of the information in this chapter assumes that you are looking at the App on your computer, however you can find all of these options on the App via your mobile phone or tablet too (though perhaps in a different order than noted here).

Let's walk through the Settings to get familiar with their contents and how you can tailor them to suit you. Select **Settings** on the App Menu to be taken to the **Settings Main Page** where we'll get started.

Device Settings

The first thing you'll see is a list of the Alexa-enabled devices that you own and that are linked to your Alexa account. The word "Online" appears beneath any device when it is currently connected to a Wi-Fi network.

Start by selecting your device from the list, and you'll be taken to a page for basic setup, organization and information:

So these are the settings for your particular device:

Wireless and Connected Devices: Click on the options here to check which Wi-Fi network your devise is on; pair your device to other

Bluetooth devices and remote controls if needed; and link to new Alexa Gadgets which are currently still in development – the idea being to link fun tech accessories with other features in the App (for example, linking and an outside bell to chime when the Alexa timer expires.)

Do Not Disturb: This feature keeps Alexa quiet including preventing incoming Calls, Messages, Drop-ins or Notifications. At any time, say, "Do not disturb," Alexa will say, "I won't disturb you." (With some Alexa-enabled devices that have screens, the screen will darken until you use the wake word again. Saying, "Turn off your screen" will work too.) Alternatively, you can toggle the Do Not Disturb on and off within the App here.

Scheduled Off: Do Not Disturb is programmable using this feature. Here's how:

- On the Alexa App, select the **Do Not Disturb** and toggle it on. Then tap or click on **Scheduled** to input the times you want the the **Do Not Disturb** to start and finish.

- If you want to change or cancel the times listed, on a PC or Mac choose Edit at the bottom and on a tablet or mobile, just tap on the time you want to change

- Note that the Do Not Disturb an only be set for daily operation; and that Alexa will continue to alert you to alarms and timers even if the Do Not Disturb is on.

Sounds: This is where you customize what sounds your device makes, when it makes them and how loud they are.

- **Alarm, Timer and Notification Volume:** Slide the bar left for lower and right for higher.

- **Audio:** The explanation of notifications is just around the corner. This allows you to determine whether a tone is given when a notification hits your Notification List. I keep Audio toggled Off unless I'm eagerly awaiting a Notification about a package being sent out for delivery or a message returned (See Calling & Messaging).

- **Custom Sounds/Alarm:** This section was covered earlier in

Reminders & Alarms, but in brief, you can select from celebrity-delivered alarm messages and custom sounds. The Default alarm shows initially; if you change it, the new choice is shown in the box.

Amazon Kids (formerly FreeTime): This is where you can enable parental controls specifically for your specific Alexa device and/or set up a subscription to the Amazon Kids+ service for more kid-friendly Alexa content, skills, games etc. You can read more about this feature in the Things to Try chapter. (Note, you can access further parental controls in the Alexa Preferences section of Settings, see below).

Device Name: You can change the name of your device here by clicking Edit and following the prompts. Note that on the mobile version of the App the Edit Name option appears under the default device name in this Device Settings section.

Device Location: I've included my complete address to get the best information about distances to restaurants and businesses near me. You don't have to enter any location, or you can input just a street and/or zip code:

- Select the Edit button.

- Input or change address information.

- Choose Save or Cancel.

Device Time Zone: To show the correct time on your device:

- Select a Region or United States from the top box to see your time zone options.

- Select the time zone you want from the lower box.

Wake Word: The default wake word is Alexa, but you can change it to Computer, Amazon or Echo. I've tried them all, and Echo is the only viable alternative for me since I often use Amazon and Computer in conversation unrelated to Alexa. Doing that creates a false "waking" of the device. If you want to change the wake word:

- In the Alexa App go to Settings > Your Echo Device > Wake Word.

- Expand the Names box with the down caret.

- Select the name you want.

- Save it, and you'll be taken to the previous page where the Wake Word will appear.

Measurement Units: If you prefer metric units for temperature and distance, toggle the buttons to On.

Device is registered to: CAUTION! When you initially set up your device your name will appear here. The note of caution relates to the option to the right Deregister. This will deregister your device, and I'm aware of only two times to do this:

- If you sell or give away the device.

- If you cannot get it to function properly in the future, Amazon recommends deregistering and reregistering it as a last resort.

Deregistering your device can also be done online, for example if you sell your device but forget to deregister it first. To deregister any device:

- Go to www.amazon.com/mycd

- Select *Your Devices*.

- Select the box to the left of the appropriate device.

- In the popup window, select *Deregister your device* and follow the prompts.

Alexa Preferences

Once you've finished with the Device Settings above click back to the main Settings page where you will find *Alexa Preferences*.

Note that on the App on your Mac or PC *Alexa Preferences* is divided into subgroups including Alexa Account and General section. There isn't this distinction in the Alexa Preferences section on the App on your mobile.

Either way, *Alexa Preferences* is where you need to go to set up various default options for a number of features, these include:

Music & Media: This section lists the accounts you've linked to Alexa, along with the user ID for the account, and those available to use with Alexa that don't require an account. If you haven't opened an account for these services or haven't yet linked your existing account to the Alexa App, you can do those by selecting any of the music services from the *Music, Video & Books* tab on the App menu. Complete instructions for the most popular music services are given in Chapter 5. Select any of the Music Services to:

• Unlink the account if you don't use the service any longer.

• Manage your account Settings by logging into your account on the service's site.

• Manage service-specific Settings such as Enabling Custom Stations, where available.

• Learn tips for using the music service.

Select the *Choose Default Music Services* option to choose a default music library and music station. For example, my libraries are Amazon Music and Spotify, and Amazon is my default. When I say, "Play Blake Shelton," Alexa plays music available on Amazon. If I want the music I have in my Spotify collection, I request it — "Play Blake Shelton from Spotify."

TV & Video: This is where you can let Alexa know your TV provider preference and then ask her questions about schedules (see more detail on this in the Things to Try chapter) and where you can link to TV provider skills to stream content to your Echo Show.

Flash Briefing: Most news services create short news summaries hourly or several times per day, in many cases to play on radio. Many of those summaries are available for playing on your Alexa-enabled device whenever you want to hear them. Most are Skills, and we've discussed Skills at length. Together, those summaries you choose make your Flash Briefing. To create yours:

• Select *Get More Flash Briefing Content*.

• Browse the list, and select the ones you want.

- Enable the Skill.

- Those you choose will be listed here.

- Toggle on those you want to play.

- Choose **Edit Order** to rearrange the order they are played.

- Say, "Play my Flash Briefing," "What's in the news" or similar, and Alexa will deliver it.

- If applicable, each news service's logo will appear on your device screen; some services include video.

- Say, "Skip" or "Next," and Alexa will move on to the next service in the briefing.

I have 11 services in my briefing, but I often hear the top story from a service and then skip to the next or skip the service altogether.

Amazon Kids (formerly FreeTime): This is the Alexa Preferences section for parental controls. This section is where you can set security features and kids profiles that will be applicable to all your Alexa-enabled devices. For parental controls that are specific to a particular Alexa device, then go to the Amazon Kids section in Device Settings (see above).

Traffic: This feature was covered in **Things to Try** chapter; your Traffic feature gives you commute times. Input a "From" location, "To" location and stops in between, if desired. Edit them to change your route, and then ask, "What's my commute?"

Sports Update: Also covered in the **Things to Try** chapter, but here's a summary. The feature allows you to follow professional teams and leagues from North America and Europe plus the football and basketball teams for most major colleges in the US:

- Use the **Search your Teams** box to find teams you want to follow.

- Click on those teams from the search results.

- They will appear in your list.

- Remove them by selecting the **X**.

- Say, "Sports Update" to hear latest scores and upcoming games for the teams in your list that are currently in season.

Calendars: Alexa can link to calendars from Google, Microsoft and Apple iCloud. Link your calendars, and add items to them with basic requests such as, "Add appointment at 3pm Thursday to my calendar" and hundreds of similar things. See Check and Manage Your Calendar in this guide's Things to Try chapter.

Lists: Alexa already manages a Shopping List and To-do List for you in the App. But you can also link your lists on Alexa to several 3rd party list apps like AnyList or Todoist:

- Create a free basic or paid premium account on one or more of those sites.

- *Select Settings > Alexa Preferences > Lists.*

- Choose a service and select Get Skill or Link Account to connect the account to Alexa.

- Sign into your Amazon account and the list service account.

- Go to the separate app of the chosen service on your phone and tap "Connect with Alexa/ Echo".

- Sign in.

- You will then see your Alexa App To-do list on your other list service, though not with all the functionality you enjoy on the Alexa App.

If you already have an account with one of those services, connecting it with Alexa might make sense. If you don't, it's redundant if you have the Alexa App on your phone.

Guard: This is where you can set up Alexa to guard your house whilst you're out! See more details about this feature in the Things to Try chapter.

Care Hub: This is where you can set up Alexa to help you stay connected to a loved one, and add options such as being alerted if your loved one calls for help. See more details about this feature in the **Things to Try** chapter.

Hunches: This is where you can disable or enable the Hunches feature that allows Alexa to help you if there's a glitch with your smart home devices. See more details about this feature in the Smart Home chapter.

Voice Responses: This is where you can toggle on or off Alexa's Brief mode, so that Alexa's responses will be briefer or substituted with a short sound; and Whisper Mode, so that you can whisper to Alexa and she can whisper back!

Voice Purchasing: The details on this topic are covered at length in *Things to Try* under "Shop Amazon (For Prime Members)". In short, Amazon Prime members with a US address and means of payment stored on Amazon can use this section to:

- Enable 1-click shopping on your Amazon account.

- Enable Voice Purchasing.

- Choose a 4-digit code and require its use with Voice Purchasing.

Household Profile: If you haven't already created an Amazon Household, clicking there will take you to Amazon so you can do so. When you create an Amazon Household, you gain four advantages:

- Members share Amazon Prime benefits when Prime Sharing is enabled.

- All digital content can be shared between adults in the household in what Amazon calls a Family Library.

- Select titles can be shared and unshared with children too.

- Payment instruments/methods can be shared with other adults in the Household.

A household can include up to two adults and four children. As we noted earlier, creating and managing an Amazon Household is done through your Amazon account. Once logged into Amazon.com:

- Hover over *Accounts & Lists* near the top of the page.

- Select "Your Account"

- In the "Shopping programs and rentals" box, select *Amazon*

Households to go to the *Manage Your Household / Your Amazon Household Benefits* page.

- Enable Prime Sharing, if desired.

- Select "*Add an Adult*," and follow the instructions including providing their login information, so they will have to give it to you or be there with you to type it in.

- And/or select "*Add a Child*," Create and Save their Profile, and follow the link to Manage Your Content and Devices to manage the content they can access.

- Adults and children can be removed just as easily, and you can "leave" a household too.

Leaving and removing can be done in this section of the App too. Select yourself, and choose Leave; select another Household member, and choose Remove. Complete information about households and how to manage yours can be found on this page: www.amazon.com/myh/manage

Create your Voice Profile (optional): You will of course know that Alexa can recognize any voice that speaks to her, but did you know that you can teach Alexa to recognize your particular voice and use that feature to link to these services for a personalized Alexa experience? Voice profiles can be set up for up to 10 people on most Alexa-enabled devices. Once you have a Voice Profile you can enjoy these enhanced features:

- Flash Briefing, Alexa will give you news updates that are linked to your personal flash briefing choices.

- Prime Music Unlimited family plan users, say "Play music" and Alexa will play music tailored to your specific Music Unlimited profile.

- Voice Purchasing, when you have a Voice Profile saved then you don't need to give Alexa your voice purchasing code to proceed with a purchase.

- Calling & Messaging, when using this features Alexa will

automatically call or message people listed only on your personal contacts.

To create your Voice Profile, simply ask Alexa to "Learn my voice", and then follow the vocal prompts from Alexa. You will be asked to repeat 10 phrases like "Alexa, order pink pajamas" and "Amazon, feed the cat". And then Alexa says, "Nice to meet you" when she's done with setting up your voice profile.

To create a Voice Profile for a different person, not listed on you account at Set Up, then first log out and sign back in to your Alexa App account, where under your name you should see the option *I'm someone else*. Click or tap on this and follow the instructions again to create a different personal profile. Then you can ask Alexa to "learn my voice" again, using the new profile.

Note that if you've already created an Amazon Household (see above) then members of the Household can say "Switch accounts" and then ask Alexa to "Learn my voice".

To delete a Voice Profile, select *Settings* > *Accounts* > *Your Voice* > *Forget my voice* and confirm.

History: Select this Setting to view your entire voice-interaction history with Alexa. Choose any line to see complete details or to delete the item. To delete all voice recordings and their associated Cards at one time:

- Go to www.amazon.com/mycd
- Select *Your Devices*.
- Select the box to the left of the appropriate device.
- In the popup window, select *Manage voice recordings*, and *Delete* or *Cancel*.

Finally, the *Settings* page also has some useful information concerning Alexa Privacy, in particular a link where you can *Manage Skills Permissions*.

14: Ressources Galore — Help & Feedback

For any voice command you read in this chapter be sure to use your wake word ("Alexa", "Amazon", etc) first.

This section of the Alexa App provides a wealth of information, though we've already covered much of it and referred to it frequently. When selecting an item from Things to Try, for example, you are usually taken here for the explanation. However, there are a few things worth mentioning about this section that haven't been covered yet in this guide.

Alexa Features – General Alexa User Guide

As you will have guessed, ***Alexa Devices and Alexa Companion Devices*** options will give you information that is particular to the specific device; we won't go into those sections in this book, but you should have a good explore if you see your Alexa-enabled device listed.

However, clicking or tapping on ***Alexa Features*** or Alexa will produce another page with further sections to explore about the Alexa App that are common to all Alexa-enabled devices, including these ones worth looking at in more detail:

Alexa Smart Home: This is where you'll get further answers for setting up, controlling and managing your smart home devices, including a useful section for troubleshooting the most common problems.

Alexa Entertainment: Lots of helpful tips to do with playing Music, Video and Audiobooks via Alexa, but sections of special interest here are:

• **Play Multi-Room Music on Echo Devices** is must-reading

if you do have more than one Echo device. There's information about using devices with the same Wake Word, which devices don't require a Wake Word (Amazon Tap, e.g.) and things you can do (like share Music between devices) and things you can't do (like play the same music on more than one device).

- We discussed voice-control of Fire TV in the Video chapter, but the Use Your **Alexa Device to Control Your Fire TV** section in the App offers more detail and will be useful for Fire TV users for linking and controlling content.

Alexa Communication: Here is your resource for Calling, Messaging and Drop-In capabilities. The information in this section and its links are comprehensive. You'll find step-by-step instructions to follow for setup and use, if what we discussed earlier isn't clear

Help Around the House with Alexa: This is where you'll find answers to questions concerning most productivity tasks such as setting alarms, timers, shopping, making lists, getting your traffic, flash briefing and calendar updates and so on.

Alexa Devices - Echo Device User Guides

To get specific information about the features of your specific Alexa enable device, you will need to return to the *Help & Feedback* homepage first then go to *Alexa Devices* where you'll find help and tips to manage features specific to your devices with further links to various help pages.

Alexa Companion Devices

This section of *Help & Feedback* is for setting up/troubleshooting companion devices such as the Echo Sub, the Echo Link Amp, the Alexa Voice Remote or using Alexa on non-Echo devices such as the Fire TV.

Contact Us

I've had no issues with Alexa that I couldn't solve using the abundance of information found in the App and on Amazon.com. Because of the good fortune I've had with Alexa, I haven't emailed or called Customer Service. However, if you have problems and can't find answers, don't hesitate to contact Amazon. Feedback is another issue. I have used the Send Feedback option seven times to date to give Amazon my thoughts on how to improve Alexa performance. I bring this up to say that Amazon has always been responsive, so if you contact the company with issues, you can expect that a customer service representative will be in touch.

Legal

If you have questions about how Amazon will use your information or what legal parameters there are for using Alexa, scanning the Legal & Compliance section will provide you with answer.

Before You Go

So, there you have it! I trust by now you have your Alexa up and running and have become familiar with many of its features. Please drop me a line at cjandersentech@gmail.com if you require any further clarification.

And finally, positive reviews on Amazon.com (https://amzn. to/3nxfNWh) make a huge difference to the success of independent authors, such as myself. If you found this guide helpful, I would be very grateful if you could take a moment to leave a review. Thank you.